INTERPRETING
THE PSALMS

Patrick D. Miller

INTERPRETING
THE PSALMS

Fortress Press   Philadelphia

Library of Congress Cataloging-in-Publication Data

Miller, Patrick D.
   Interpreting the Psalms.

   Bibliography: p.
   Includes index.
   1. Bible. O.T. Psalms—Criticism, interpretation,
etc. I. Title.
   BS1430.2.M48   1986   223'.206   85–16258
   ISBN 0–8006–1896–3

Printed in the United States of America   1-1896

01   00   99   98   97   7   8   9   10   11   12   13   14   15   16

CONTENTS

PREFACE

The psalms of the Old Testament belong to the earliest memories of my childhood when our family would gather on Sunday afternoons to read, memorize, and sing them. It was not an occasion that my sisters and I particularly relished. When we were given the opportunity to choose a psalm to memorize or read, invariably we chose Psalm 117 or Psalm 133, for the obvious reason of brevity—besides, we were fascinated with the oil running down Aaron's beard! The lessons, however, took. Not only have the psalms been present on family occasions through the years—trips, marriages, deaths—as they have been for countless other family circles, but they have become for me both an important part of the corporate worship of the people of God and a central preoccupation in my study and teaching of the Old Testament. Worship with the psalms and study of the psalms came especially close together during a sabbatical year in Cambridge, England. I frequently attended morning worship or evensong in the college chapels and heard the psalms beautifully sung in cycle; at the same time most of my hours in the study were spent with the psalms.

It is in the conviction that the psalms belong both at the center of the life and worship of Christian congregations and in the midst of the personal pilgrimage that each of us makes under the shadow of the Almighty, that I have written this book. Its audience is most obviously pastors and teachers in the church as well as those who may not have such official functions but love to read and study the psalms for whatever light they have to shed on their way in the world.

Part 1 of the book is designed to help interpreters of the psalms find entrée into them in various ways, to hear their theological claims and to discern their point of contact with human life. Chapter 1 presents and assays some of the main things that are happening in the scholarly study of the psalms. Here I have tried neither to cover the field nor merely to report but to identify issues and approaches that seem to me to matter or be of consequence for the church's faithful hearing of the psalms and the interpreter's task in that enterprise. A number of issues touched on there feed into later chapters.

Chapters 2, 4, and 5 focus on hermeneutical and theological approaches to the psalms. Chapter 2 seeks to identify ways in which the psalms are very open to a continuing lively resonance with the issues and questions of human existence under God. Or put another way, I have suggested some handles to help the interpreter grab hold of the psalms—or to help others find a handhold through the psalms. That effort continues in chapter 4, where I suggest that the biblical laments, which are found principally in the Psalter, are open-ended both ways, that is, forward and backward. They touch so obviously on dimensions that are common to all human experience, present as well as past, that for the most part we do not have to perform hermeneutical contortions to "make them relevant"; but they also can be illumined and illustrated by hearing them against the narratives and stories of the Old Testament that are themselves reflective of the rich variety and the heights and depths of human experience. Chapter 5 moves to the hymns and songs of the Psalter, and the Old Testament generally, to try to uncover their central theological themes and reverberations. Praise and thanksgiving turn us from our self-preoccupation to focus upon the one who is Lord of life. Interpreting the hymns of praise is primarily an enterprise of seeing, by means of their words, the glory and majesty of that Lord and being drawn into the chorus of praise.

Chapter 3 is probably less common in a book of this sort than the other chapters. It deals with the poetry of the psalms, a matter that is usually treated in commentaries and introductions to the psalms but nearly always apart from hermeneutical concerns. As one can see by looking at more classical or older treatments of hermeneutics, however, that has not always been the case. The form of the psalms is not separable from their content. That has long been recognized with regard to some formal characteristics, for example, genre or type, but it is equally true with regard to their poetic features. So I have tried to suggest some ways and give some illustrations of how attention to poetic features can aid in hearing and understanding the psalms.

Part 2 of this volume consists of ten expositions of psalms. Here many of the points made in Part 1 are illustrated, though not mechanically, I hope, or in a way that suggests there are certain moves one always makes to appropriate the communication of the psalms for preaching and teaching. I hope one encounters the liveliness and individuality of each psalm as well as the applicability of some of the handles suggested earlier. The psalms chosen for Part 2 were not selected primarily because they fit the categories of the earlier discussion. For example, none of the expositions take up a particular hymn, although chapter 4 deals with several hymns. And some of the psalms chosen for this part (for example, Psalm 82) do not neatly fit into any of the modes suggested earlier. All the psalms in Part 2 are, in my judgment, texts of large significance that belong to any preaching and teaching of the psalms in the community of faith. The expositions seek to show why that is so, and the directions suggested in Part 1 are pursued in the interpretive enterprise as these psalms are taken up. It may be that some readers of the volume will find one or two of the expositions the most useful part of the book.

It should be pointed out that the chapters are interrelated and flow out of one another, but they are also capable of being read discretely. Indeed some of them appeared in an earlier form as separate essays (see below). If, for example, a reader wants to look at how one might treat the laments, she or he may read chapter 4, where reference is made to other parts of the book that are related or illustrative, without presupposing that one must go back and read all the preceding or continue through the rest of the book. In that sense each chapter stands on its own and can be read on its own. This involves in some instances intentional reiteration of points made in other chapters, in a manner that, I hope, is not merely repetitious.

Some annotated bibliographical suggestions are given at the end. I have selected some resources I believe can be helpful for teaching and preaching the psalms. Many excellent works are left out, including all foreign-language studies. A number of these may be found in the notes to the various chapters.

Where passages from the Old Testament are quoted, I have used the RSV text or my own translation. Verses are cited according to the numbering of the English text. Those who use the Hebrew text can easily find the verse or verses under discussion.

Some of the chapters and two of the expositions in this book are revisions of material that appeared in an earlier form elsewhere: chapter 1 in

Word and World 5 (1985): 132–143; part of chapter 3 in *Vetus Testamentum* 29 (1979): 416–24; chapter 4 in *Interpretation* 37 (1983): 32–45; chapter 5 in *Interpretation* 39 (1985): 5–19; the exposition of Psalm 127 in *Journal for the Study of the Old Testament* 22 (1982): 119–32; and the exposition of Psalm 130 in *Interpretation* 33 (1979): 176–80. Permission to use the above materials has been granted by the publishers.

I want to express my gratitude to Nancy Berman for her efficient preparation of the manuscript and for her grace under pressure.

This book is dedicated first of all to Lila Bonner Miller, M.D., who first taught me to sing the psalms and who knows, far more than I shall ever comprehend, the power and meaning of these songs and prayers in life and death, sickness and health, faith and doubt, sorrow and joy. I dedicate these pages also to Mary Miller Brueggemann and Belle Miller Mc-Master, who were with me in the family circle when we first began to learn the psalms.

PART ONE
General Approaches

1. CURRENT ISSUES IN THE INTERPRETATION OF THE PSALMS

Every individual interpretation of the psalms is a part of and builds upon a larger context of many such efforts. We begin, therefore, with a look at some of the main currents that are currently shaping the study of the psalms and at least in part the directions set forth in the pages that follow. No effort is made to cover the larger discussion exhaustively here. My focus will be on those issues that seem to me to be at the forefront, and of potential importance for persons whose primary task is the interpretation of the psalms within the life of the community of faith.

THE FUNCTION OF THE PSALMS IN ANCIENT ISRAEL

Form-critical study of the psalms has dominated, if not controlled, the way in which this part of Scripture has been handled during this century—a fact that is as evident in popular treatments of the psalms and commentaries as it is in the scholarly literature. Attention to the type and character of the psalms, with an effort to understand how they functioned in the life and worship of individual and community, can offer either direct clues or heuristic suggestions for their continuing role in personal piety and public worship (see chap. 2). The very character of the psalms, however, as relatively brief individual units, for the most part now loosed from any context but the literary one, means that the many questions about the type and especially about the setting in life of the various types are uncertain of answer or open to various answers.

The basic schema set forth by Hermann Gunkel and Joachim Begrich in their introduction to the psalms[1] remains the foundation on which others continue to build. The most important comprehensive treatment since their study is found in the work of Claus Westermann.[2] He has made a very strong case for seeing praise and lament as the two poles of human address to God and as by far the dominant categories of the psalms. With regard to the first pole, praise, the primary issue raised by Westermann and debated by others is whether or not there is any separate category of thanksgiving to God that can be distinguished from praise of God—either in Hebrew thought generally or in the types of psalms—as Gunkel indicated in separating the song of thanksgiving from the hymn of praise. Westermann argues that both categories in the Psalter are distinct from expressions of thanks in the human sphere in that they are totally directed toward God and seek to exalt God by persons who in spontaneous joy think not of themselves but only of God.

The dimension of thanksgiving need not be played down in the Psalter or in Hebrew thought generally. It is clear that expressions of blessing toward human beings and toward God, as well as the more explicit declarations of praise, express gratitude as well as exalting God and bearing testimony to the Lord's grace and power (see chap. 4). Westermann is correct, however, in identifying *praise* as the primary category, and in fact he essentially preserves Gunkel's distinction in differentiating *tĕhillāh* (Gunkel = hymn; Westermann = descriptive praise) and *tôdāh* (Gunkel = song of thanksgiving; Westermann = recounting or narrative praise). The latter category explicitly represents psalms that praise God by making joyful response to God's deliverance of persons from distress, in distinction from those that praise God more generally for majesty and creative power. The discussion is not unimportant for thinking theologically about the nature of praise and its relationship to thanksgiving and confession or proclamation, all of which have to do with what goes on in the *tôdāh*.[3]

The lament or complaint psalms in the Psalter and elsewhere in the Old Testament have been the subject of even more attention than the psalms of praise. Various proposals have been put forth to try to explain the situation and purpose of the laments of individuals. These represent efforts to understand who the speaker (the "I") is in the individual laments, who the enemies are, and what the human need is. Related to

---

1. Hermann Gunkel and Joachim Begrich, *Einleitung in die Psalmen* (Göttingen: Vandenhoeck & Ruprecht, 1933). For a brief summary see Hermann Gunkel, *The Psalms* (Philadelphia: Fortress Press, Facet Books, 1967).
2. Claus Westermann, *Praise and Lament in the Psalms* (Atlanta: John Knox Press, 1981).
3. On the praise of God in the psalms, see chap. 5.

such questions is the matter of the cultic character of these psalms. References in various psalms to the sanctuary, sacrifice, help in the morning, and purification suggest a cultic connection. But is that universally the case, and does the ritual activity that may be associated with the laments take place in public cult or worship, or does it happen privately, perhaps in the context of the family? Some interpreters have noted and emphasized those places in the psalms that seem to identify the speaker as a person who has been accused of something. Noting places in the Old Testament where legal cases could be handled at the sanctuary (e.g., Exod. 22:8–9; Deut. 17:8–13; 19:15–21; 21:1–9; 1 Kings 8:31–32), Hans Schmidt suggested that a number of individual laments arise out of the language and activity of a sacral judicial procedure in the sanctuary in which one who claimed to be falsely accused prayed to God against his or her enemies (accusers) and received from the priests the verdict of God, which if favorable then elicited a further prayer of thanksgiving. Examples of this are Psalms 3, 4, 5, 7, 17, 26, 27, 54, 55, and 69.[4] Walter Beyerlin more recently has proposed a modification of this view, seeing in a number of psalms (e.g., Psalms 4, 5, 7, 11, 17, 23, 26, 27, 57, and 63) a plea for divine judgment that is not understood as threatening or tied to a regularized sacral procedure in which the accused is brought to the priests for judgment, but that is a protection. The sanctuary provided asylum.[5] More sweepingly L. Delekat has proposed that these psalms, along with many others, are prayers of persons seeking asylum in the sanctuary, who wrote a short prayer for help on the temple wall, probably in the evening upon arrival. After the certainty of a hearing had been received, a short note to that effect was added. In time, according to Delekat, the prayers became longer and more artful. They could be engraved on a stele and perhaps by one who had not composed the prayer.[6]

Neither Schmidt nor Beyerlin would ascribe all the laments to an occasion of judicial procedure or protection from false accusers in the sanctuary. They both have acknowledged that a number of laments seem to cry out not for divine justice but for deliverance from sickness and misery (e.g., Psalms 6, 13, 22, 28, 38, and 102)—a view accentuated earlier by Sigmund Mowinckel and affirmed by Gunkel as probably the origin

---

4. Hans Schmidt, *Das Gebet des Angeklagten im Alten Testament* (Giessen, 1928).
5. Walter Beyerlin, *Die Rettung der Bedrängten in den Feindpsalmen der Einzelnen auf institutionelle Zusammenhänge untersucht* (Göttingen: Vandenhoeck & Ruprecht, 1970).
6. L. Delekat, *Asylie und Schutzorakel am Zionheiligtum* (Leiden: E. J. Brill, 1967). For possible examples of inscribed psalms, see P. D. Miller, "Psalms and Inscriptions," *Congress Volume, Vienna 1980*, ed. J.A. Emerton (Leiden: E. J. Brill, 1981), 311–32.

of some of the psalms before they were loosed from their cultic setting. More recently this view has been elaborated by Klaus Seybold:

> According to these texts, the psalm of the individual sick person was variously anchored in the lament phase and was a prayer for preservation and healing. In keeping with this context, it was often simultaneously a confession of guilt and a request for mercy, spoken within the private sickroom, probably with the aid of a priest. It was very likely not performed by the sick person himself during a pilgrimage to a holy place, since anyone seriously sick was generally not up to the rigors of such a trip. Or the psalm belonged in the thanksgiving phase as a laudatory prayer and personal (sacrificial) contribution within the framework of a community meal celebrated at the sanctuary after successful recovery and as part of the reconciliation and rehabilitation of the recovered person. This could happen . . . "twice, three times" during the course of life. The actual, individual, and liturgically formed psalms of sickness originated in this way.[7]

The most impressive proposal in recent years for understanding the form and function of the individual laments is that of Erhard Gerstenberger, whose analysis is shaped by three contributing factors that have not played so large a role in other interpretations: *(a)* sociological analysis of the relation of the individual to the group and of the function of the group in society as well as of the relation between word and act in ritual matters; *(b)* the everyday scheme of prayer as uncovered in the *narrative* texts of the Old Testament; and *(c)* Mesopotamian ritual texts.[8] The result of his investigation is to place the individual laments outside the official cult and the temple. These laments belong rather to healing ceremonies within the circle of the family. A person who may be threatened by any of a wide range of troubles goes to a ritual expert within the family or clan—someone trained in the ritual but not a priest—participates in a healing rite involving both words and actions, and gets rid of the threat or trouble. The final goal and consequence of such activity is the rehabilitation of the individual as a member of his or her small group or primary social sphere—clan or family—and thus the restoration of clan harmony.

If all this sounds more like family or group therapy than prayer and worship in the church, that is neither surprising nor accidental. In his concluding remarks, Gerstenberger, noting the increasing isolation of

7. Klaus Seybold and Ulrich B. Mueller, *Sickness and Healing*, Biblical Encounter Series (Nashville: Abingdon Press, 1981), 44. Seybold's more elaborate development of this view appears in *Das Gebet des Kranken im Alten Testament* (Stuttgart: W. Kohlhammer, 1973).
8. Erhard Gerstenberger, *Der bittende Mensch* (Neukirchen-Vluyn: Neukirchener Verlag, 1980).

individuals in a modern technological society, compares the rehabilitation of the sufferer in the Old Testament to contemporary group-therapy movements that seek to reintegrate a distressed person into the primary group through a process of words and actions under a group leader who is an expert in the process of "ritual."[9] In this same connection Gerstenberger sees in Old Testament scholarship's inability to think about these matters except in terms of individual prayer and piety or the official and corporate worship of the people a reflection of the Protestant tendency to understand prayer as either an individual matter or a part of public worship. The lament psalms are an indication of the fact that individuals live their lives "above all in the small world of the primary group" (translation mine) rather than in the larger—albeit secondary, when viewed sociologically—sphere of community of people. It is in the small group that meaning is found and religion experienced.[10]

Gerstenberger's analysis, which has impressed many, will continue to be tested and modified. His work is at least a challenge to others to assess theologically the sociological reality of the significance for human existence of small groups (e.g., families, circles of friends, groups with common interest or needs) as the context for meaningful existence. With regard both to Gerstenberger's work on the lament psalms and to the contemporary experience of church and synagogue, the relation of these smaller groups to the larger spheres (e.g., church, community, nation) that give identity and evoke loyalty remains to be developed.[11]

It would not do to characterize major approaches to the understanding of the laments without recognizing that the view of H. Birkeland,[12]

---

9. Ibid., 167–69.
10. Ibid.
11. A similar point of view has been set forth in two works by Westermann's student Rainier Albertz: *Weltschöpfung und Menschenschöpfung* (Stuttgart: Calwer, 1974) and *Persönliche Frömmigkeit und offizielle Religion* (Stuttgart: Calwer, 1978). Unlike the laments of the people, which are rooted in the history of salvation and thus associated with the official theology of the nation, the individual laments are rooted in the history of the individual and that person's relationship with God. They belong, therefore, according to Albertz, to the personal religion that has its locus in the sphere of the small group and the family. The lament is an appeal to one's personal God to be present and protect and is intended to rehabilitate and restore the person to the small group. In a long conclusion to the second work, Albertz suggests some implications of this perspective for the focus of ministry. He sees ministry involved more in the family and its life and worship, helping to give family members a better understanding of themselves and their situation as well as to actualize and strengthen in each new phase or turning point in life their personal relationship of trust in God (*Persönliche Frömmigkeit*, 208). In his treatment of the biblical material, Albertz gives some attention to the integration of the personal religion of the individual in the small group into the official religion and worship of the larger community.
12. H. Birkeland, *The Evildoers in the Book of Psalms* (Oslo, 1955).

and later Mowinckel[13] and others, that the "I" of the laments is the king acting in behalf of or as representative of the people in crying out for help against national enemies, has been taken up afresh and impressively by J. H. Eaton, who sees some fifty-odd psalms of the individual as being in fact royal psalms.[14] Such a construal of the texts is plausible and is undergirded by the centrality of the king in ancient Israel, and possibly in the official cult, as well as by the ascription of so many psalms to David. The connection of the psalms to the Messiah and the christological use of them by the early church would be even more direct should such an interpretation be on the right track.

The search for a readily identifiable situation as the context for understanding the laments may, however, be illusory or unnecessary. The language of these psalms with its stereotypical, generalizing, and figurative style is so open-ended that later readers, on the one hand, are stopped from peering behind them to one or more clearly definable sets of circumstances or settings in life, and on the other hand, are intentionally set free to adapt them to varying circumstances and settings. Indeed one can do that in relating some of the laments to persons and events in the Old Testament even though the psalms did not *originally* belong to such persons' experience in the sense of being composed by them or for them; this is a way of interpreting the laments that is spelled out in a later chapter.[15] Gunkel, Westermann, and others have helped us see the distinction between original purpose and later use even when we may not be absolutely certain about either one.[16] Indeed in the work of Westermann, the laments are not at all seen in the context of cultic and ritual activity but are seen as one of the primary modes of prayer (the other being praise) that characterize human address to God.[17]

---

13. Sigmund Mowinckel, *The Psalms in Israel's Worship* (Oxford: Basil Blackwell, 1962), esp. chap. 3, 7, and 8.

14. John H. Eaton, *Kingship and the Psalms* (London: SCM Press, 1976). See his commentary cited in the bibliography at the end of the present work.

15. See chap. 4.

16. With regard to the prevalence of interpretations that focus upon sickness and false accusation as the primary conditions of the lamenters, Joachim Becker's summary words are appropriate:

> It is no accident that sickness and accusation dominate in the prayer speech of the individual lament songs. These have to do with the two fundamental human needs. Sickness is the threatening of physical existence by lessening life. The sick person in the Old Testament believes himself or herself to be near the entrance to the realm of the dead. Accusation is the threatening of moral existence in the community and no less dangerous. (J. Becker, *Wege der Psalmenexegese* [Stuttgart: Katholisches Bibelwerk, 1975], 33; trans. mine)

17. Westermann, *Praise and Lament*, 15–35.

Theological concerns come very much to the fore in Westermann's analysis of the laments when compared with other treatments. Two issues that have theological implications stand out in the current discussion. One of these is what seems to be a simple question: How are we to label the genre under discussion? Should these psalms be called laments or complaints (*Klage Anklage*), or should one designate them petitions or supplications (*Bitte*)? Westermann is a good example of the former designation, Gerstenberger, the latter, though each uses the other terminology also. While this may seem to be simply another case of form critics unable to agree on standard terminology, it is really more than that. At least to some extent the decision represents a judgment as to whether one regards such prayer as functioning primarily to lay out complaint against God and others, articulating the human need, and giving form to the anguish and despair of one in trouble,[18] or whether one sees these prayers as serving to place before God specific petitions for help in the hope and expectation that God will intervene in the situation to deliver one from trouble. Clearly both dimensions are present in the lament psalms, but the accent one places, or discerns, may affect one's theology. The emphasis may tend to create an understanding of prayer as an expression of human distress and a struggle with God that is in itself healing and restorative, and a notion of God as present and involved in suffering more than delivering persons out of it. Or one's sense of these prayers as petitions for help may focus one's theology on prayer as effective in bringing about the power of God, who is able to deliver and does so. It is of course possible also that the theology of prayer held by the interpreter of these psalms may shape the way the genres are understood. If the Passion of Jesus, that is, God's incarnational com-passion with a suffering humanity (see the expositions of Psalms 14 and 22 below), and God's resurrection of the crucified Jesus are any clue, we would seem to be compelled to try to hold complaint and petition together.[19]

A second theological issue that may be identified in the ongoing study of the lament psalms is the question of how they identify the fundamental human need. Traditionally these psalms have been seen as reflecting

18. See Samuel Balentine, *The Hidden God: The Hiding of the Face of God in the Old Testament* (London: Oxford Univ. Press, 1983).

19. Both the modern consciousness vis-à-vis the intervention of God in the nexus of events and the loosing of the lament psalms from a possible highly specific cultic event to a more spiritual setting in the ongoing experience of worship and piety have probably contributed to an emphasis upon the complaint character of these psalms more than their character as petitions for help.

the human condition of sinfulness before God, a condition that is directly attested in the so-called penitential psalms (Psalms 6, 32, 38, 51, 102, 130, and 143) and inferred from the association between sickness and sin and judgment that may be discerned in various Old Testament contexts. In contemporary interpretation of the psalms, that view is being recognized as much too simple, if not misleading. Most of the psalms either do not identify the plight of the lamenter with sin or at least are ambiguous on that score. Westermann again is one who has addressed some of the theological implications of this fact by suggesting that Pauline theology has shifted the lament of the suffering one to the confession of the sinner. As he suggests, this shift has had large ramifications for Christian theology's understanding of the work of Christ. The focus has been on Jesus' work of salvation's having to do with the forgiveness of sins rather than ending human suffering, even though the Gospels offer the Old Testament lament, especially Psalm 22, as a reference point for understanding the Passion of Jesus, that is, his identification with the suffering of those who cry out in the laments (see the exposition of Psalm 22 in Part 2).

More recently Samuel Balentine has demonstrated that while the motif of the hiding of the face of God, and related themes, such as God's rejecting, forgetting, being silent, and the like, are frequently understood as manifestations of divine judgment for sin when appearing in prophetic texts, that is not the case in the psalms. There such expressions reflect more a sense of doubt, despair, and alienation from God, a condition that is frequently quite inexplicable, as is evidenced by the occasional protestations of innocence, protestations that are hardly congruent with a Pauline anthropology.[20] Most Christian readers have about as much difficulty with these claims of innocence as they do with the imprecations against enemies—in both cases because they cut against the grain of what is heard from the New Testament. It might seem that the communal laments of the people would be primarily cries for forgiveness of sin rather than pleas for help, but that assumption also may be a reflection of a prophetic-Christian reading of the texts. Murray Haar has demonstrated that these psalms subordinate the issue of sin to the claim on the covenantal relationship with God, which means that God's fate is bound up with that of Israel, and the enemies of Israel are the enemies of God. Confession of sin is not a prominent feature of the communal laments (Psalms 44, 60, 74, 79, 80, 83, and 89).[21]

20. See n. 8 above.
21. Murray Haar, "The God-Israel Relationship in the Community Lament Psalms" (Diss., Union Theological Seminary in Virginia, 1985).

Before leaving the issue of the form and function of the psalms, one should note the stimulating hermeneutical efforts in this area on the part of Walter Brueggemann. A decade ago he laid out the lament-deliverance relationship as a basic structure of Israel's faith that is not only prominent in the psalms but runs throughout the Old Testament.[22] Subsequently Brueggemann placed the lament psalms over against the analysis by Elizabeth Kübler-Ross of the death-grief process that she discovered in her work with terminally ill patients. Brueggemann thus highlighted the significance of form and structure for persons handling loss, grief, and death, while underscoring some of the distinctiveness of the process in the community that is formed by faith.[23] The most extensive overall treatment of the form and function of the psalms on Brueggemann's part has been a very heuristic proposal, growing out of the work of Paul Ricoeur, that the psalms speak to or from situations of *orientation* (esp. hymns), *disorientation* or *dislocation* (laments), and *reorientation* (esp. songs of thanksgiving or declarative praise).[24] In all of this Brueggemann draws together psychological and hermeneutical strands in ways that suggest points of reference for a contemporary reading of the psalms.

REINTERPRETATION OF THE PSALMS

While the term "reinterpretation" is not fully adequate, it does point to an aspect of psalms study that focuses more on the final form of a psalm than its original genre and character. A number of psalms are in some fashion composite, or the result of earlier psalms, or parts of psalms being reinterpreted in a new time. The result is often very different from the original form and function, but the dynamic that is present in the psalms' capacity to speak in and for different situations is well illustrated in the very growth of the Psalter itself. Many of the psalms are perceived to be the result of scribal activity in exilic and post-exilic times and to be impacted more by concerns of wisdom and torah and the search for true piety than by the influence of the cult. Some of these psalms have been described as anthologies (e.g., Psalms 25, 33, 34, 103, 111, 112, 119, and 145)[25] because they are created by drawing upon

---

22. Walter Brueggemann, "From Hurt to Joy, From Death to Life," *Interpretation* 28 (1974): 3–19.

23. Walter Brueggemann, "The Formfulness of Grief," *Interpretation* 31 (1977): 263–75.

24. Walter Brueggemann, "Psalms and the Life of Faith: A Suggested Typology of Function," *Journal for the Study of the Old Testament* 17 (1980): 3–32. See Brueggemann's *The Message of the Psalms: A Theological Commentary* (Minneapolis: Augsburg Pub. House, 1984).

25. Becker, *Wege der Psalmenexegese*, 75.

pieces, expressions, verses, and language of other psalms—as well as other Old Testament traditions—that were composed not only earlier but possibly for quite specific cultic occasions. Here expressions for "seeking the Lord," "fearing God," and God as "refuge," as well as references to the afflicted, the poor, and the like, which may have originally had in mind the condition, need, and activities of persons in poverty or oppressed by others, have been spiritualized to describe the state of the pious Israelite before God.[26]

Such literary creations expressive of a torah piety are clearly present in the Psalter. Indeed one can identify obvious use of certain psalms in the composition of other psalms, for example, in the relationships between Psalms 18 and 144 or Psalms 115 and 135 (the latter pair drawing on a number of psalm texts as well as other Old Testament material), the identity of Psalm 70 with Ps. 40:14–18, and the composition of Psalm 108 out of Pss. 57:8–12 and 60:7–14, as well as 1 Chronicles 16 out of Pss. 105:1–15; 96:1–13; and 106:1, 47–48. The issue that remains the subject of debate, however, is how far one can go in assigning psalms to this process in which composition grows out of the concerns identified above. The language is so stereotyped that one may claim an early lament as a later spiritualized creation when that may not be the case at all. Nevertheless, enough clear examples exist that one may believe the foundations to have been laid for an ongoing process of reinterpreting the psalms.

Another aspect of the reinterpretation that went on in the formation of the Psalter is the transformation of individual psalms possibly from the pre-exilic era, into psalms of the community in the exilic and post-exilic periods. The "I" of these individual psalms became Israel when the psalms were edited and rewritten at a later period. That process was not mechanical and nonsubstantive. To the contrary, the psalms were given a new meaning in a new time. Joachim Becker has been one of the primary advocates of such an understanding of the psalms, seeing a significant number of them as examples of reworking to give a new interpretation in a new time (Psalms 9, 10, 22, 40, 45, 54, 56, 59, 66, 68, 69, 85, 93, 102, 107, 108, and 118.)[27] For Becker the most noticeable form of the

---

26. See the summary discussion of ibid., chap. 9, and the works by A. Deissler, A. Gelin, and A. Robert that are referred to there.

27. In addition to Becker's *Wege der Psalmenexegese*, one should consult his more extended study, *Israel deutet seine Psalmen: Urform und Neuinterpretation in den Psalmen* (Stuttgart: Katholisches Bibelwerk, 1975).

new interpretation is the transformation of original cultic songs of lament and thanksgiving into eschatological songs reflecting the exilic or post-exilic situation of Israel in its conflicts with its neighbors.[28] He sees four central ideas in the eschatological salvation word of these psalms: God, whose power is revealed in creation and deliverance from exile, enters into rule and appears on Zion; deliverance from exile, return, and renewal as a people occupy a central place; the nations recognize the saving act of God, assemble to worship on Zion, and are punished and destroyed; Israel's posterity shall possess the land and shall inherit the blessing.[29]

A further mode of new interpretation that has been recognized for a long time but that is also the subject of current interest is the historicizing of the psalms, a feature primarily introduced by the titles that were added to the psalms, associating them primarily with David and his life and experiences.[30] Such ascriptions served not only to identify a presumed author but to provide some hermeneutical clue to understanding the psalms thus titled.[31] Such historicizing, however, was not confined to the process of adding titles, according to Becker. For example, an individual song of thanksgiving in Ps. 18:2–21 became a royal song of David with the addition of vv. 32–51 and the title. The whole was then placed into the David story (2 Samuel 22). One can cite other examples of psalms that have been historicized by being ascribed to figures in the biblical story—for example, 1 Sam. 2:1–10 (Hannah), Isa. 38:10–20 (Hezekiah), and Jonah 2:3–10 (Jonah).[32]

---

28. Cf. B. S. Childs, *Introduction to the Old Testament as Scripture* (Philadelphia: Fortress Press, 1979), 517–18.

29. Becker, *Wege der Psalmenexegese*, 93ff.

30. See Becker, *Wege der Psalmenexegese*, chap. 12; Childs, *Introduction*, 520–22; and chap. 4 of this book.

31. Childs sees this interpretive move as follows:

[T]he incidents chosen as evoking the Psalms were not royal occasions or representative of the kingly office. Rather David is pictured simply as a man, indeed chosen by God for the sake of all Israel, but who displays all the strengths and weakness of all human beings. He emerges as a person who experiences the full range of human emotions, from fear and despair to courage and love, from complaint and plea to praise and thanksgiving. . . . The effect of this new context has wide hermeneutical implications. The psalms are transmitted as the sacred psalms of David, but they testify to all the common troubles and joys of ordinary human life in which all persons participate. (p. 521)

Cf. M. Fishbane, "Torah and Tradition," in *Tradition and Theology in the Old Testament*, ed. D. A. Knight (Philadelphia: Fortress Press, 1977), 287; and Miller, "Psalms and Inscriptions."

32. Becker, *Israel*, 33.

THE PSALTER AS A COLLECTION

The interest in the way various psalms may have been edited and given a new interpretation in the exilic and post-exilic age has contributed to a growing appreciation of the Psalter as a *collection* or *book* of psalms. Both the process of formation and the significance of the final shape of the Psalter have been matters of debate or discussion. Investigations of smaller collections and interrelationships among the psalms have suggested a more conscious composition of the whole than has been sometimes recognized. Klaus Seybold has done a very careful study of the psalms of ascents (Psalms 120—134) to show that they are interrelated not only by a common title, Songs of Ascents, but by linguistic expressions, content, theology, and redactional activity. He has seen them arising out of a lay context but collected together as a kind of handbook of songs and prayers for pilgrims to Zion. They reflect a communal orientation that affirms the close relation to God and rejoices in Zion as God's chosen abode.[33] Pierre Auffret has tried to demonstrate the interrelationships of Psalms 120—134 by analysis of literary structure and has also suggested that Psalms 135—138 are a consciously constructed group that have clear relation to Psalms 120—134, and more daringly, that Psalms 15—24 are a group arranged chiastically around Psalm 19 as a center.[34]

Westermann has identified several features of the present shape of the Psalter, including the grouping, to some extent, of psalms according to distinctions that have been recognized form-critically.[35] There are groupings of psalms that are primarily individual (e.g., the David psalms) and some that are largely psalms of the community (in the Korah and Asaph psalms as well as the Songs of Ascents). The lament psalms occur more in the first half of the Psalter and hymns of praise more in the latter—a literary movement from dominant strains of lament to dominant shouts of praise that reflects a basic theological structure as well as the movement encountered in individual laments. Westermann has also suggested that the original Psalter may have been Psalms 1—119, to which the Songs of Ascents and others were added.[36] Whether or not that can be proved, it is clear from the begin-

---

33. K. Seybold, *Die Wallfahrtspsalmen* (Neukirchen-Vluyn: Neukirchener Verlag, 1978).
34. P. Auffret, *La sagesse à bati sa maison: Etudes de structures littéraires dans l'Ancien Testament et specialment dans les Psaumes* (Fribourg: Editions Universitaires, 1982), 407–549.
35. Westermann, *Praise and Lament*, 250–58.
36. Ibid.

ning and ending of the Psalter that some guides have been given for understanding the whole. Psalms 1 and 2 form an introduction that suggests, first, that one finds here a true torah piety that will show the way to go for those who love the Lord and the law, and second, that these psalms also show the way of God's rule over the larger human communities (see the expositions of Psalms 1 and 2 in Part 2). The conclusion to the psalms, that is, Psalm 150, and the title of the Psalter (tĕhillîm, "hymns") give the Psalter to the community as a book of praise to God (see chap. 4).

The appearance of a number of psalms manuscripts at Qumran, including the large psalms scroll from cave 11 with a decidedly different order and arrangement of the psalms that are on it, has raised the issue of whether or not there may have been another authoritative or canonical Psalter than the one that currently exists in the Hebrew Bible—one that could have been a genuine rival or alternative to the form preserved in the Masoretic text.[37] While the matter is hardly settled, the evidence tends toward the conclusion that the Qumran manuscripts are dependent on the received canonical Psalter of the Hebrew Bible. The cave 11 psalms scroll (11QPs[a]), which contains only the latter third of the Psalter, is where the most variation occurs, both in reordering and in the inclusion of noncanonical psalms. But over two-thirds of the psalms manuscripts or fragments show only canonical materials extant and in the expected sequence.[38] The grouping of Psalms 105, 95, and 106 in 1 Chronicles 16 shows us both that book 4 of the Psalter already existed as a unit (because the conclusion to that book, which follows the end of Psalm 106, is included in 1 Chron. 16:36) and that psalms from the canonical text could be regrouped for liturgical purposes. It may be that the unusual contents and ordering of 11QPs[a] reflect liturgical concerns as well as the desire to create "a library edition of the putative works of David."[39] Patrick Skehan was probably correct in his judgment that we cannot learn anything from the Qumran texts about "the formative period of the building up of the standard collection of 150 psalms."[40]

---

37. J. A. Sanders, "Cave 11 surprises and the Question of Canon," *McCormick Quarterly* 21 (1968): 1–15; idem, *The Dead Sea Psalms Scroll* (Ithaca, N.Y.: Cornell Univ. Press, 1967), 14.

38. P. W. Skehan, "Qumran and Old Testament Criticism," in *Qumran: Sa Piété, sa théologie et son milieu*, ed. M. Delcor (Louvain: Louvain Univ. Press, 1978), 167.

39. Ibid., 169.

40. Ibid., 164.

LITERARY STUDY OF THE PSALTER

In conclusion, one should be aware that the growing interest in the literary study of the Bible has had its impact also on the study of the psalms in two ways. First, there is the renewed and intense interest in trying to define the nature and character of Hebrew poetry, with particular attention to the poetic line and its function in building larger blocks. The question whether or not meter exists in Hebrew poetry, or can be described if it does exist, remains much debated.[41] The phenomenon of parallelism has been the subject of major treatment in recent years. Stephen Geller has proposed a system for analysis of aspects of parallelism that sets up some basic categories and applies the concept of grammatical paradigm to produce a reconstructed sentence out of poetic couplets.[42] In a somewhat different direction, James Kugel claims that parallelism is not a poetic device that breaks down into many types but is essentially a way of heightening, reinforcing, or—to use his term—"seconding" a point or statement made in the first colon of a poetic line.[43] The most complex recent proposal about the nature of Hebrew poetry is that of Michael O'Connor, who combines analysis of lines on a syntactical basis with the examination of various tropes or figures as the way to approach small numbers of lines, that is, bicola and tricola.[44] These studies raise the question whether parallelism in Hebrew poetry is one thing (Kugel) or many (Geller and O'Connor). They effectively rule out the usual handbook approach that suggests all lines can be seen in terms of three types of parallelism (synonymous, antithetic, and synthetic). While I have found Kugel's approach particularly helpful in analyzing poetry and draw upon it in chapter 3, it is also the case that both Geller and O'Connor provide categories that, when applied to lines of poetry, give us handles for grasping both logical and aesthetic dimensions of Hebrew poetry.

Beyond the focus on parallelism and the nature of Hebrew poetry, which of course encompasses much more than simply the psalms, there is a second way in which the growing interest in literary study of the Bible has left its mark on the understanding of the psalms. Literary study of the Psalter has sought to apply stylistic and rhetorical analysis, in which the issues of formation and function are less to the fore, and the

---

41. See, for example, James Barr's review of J. Kugel's *The Idea of Biblical Poetry* in *The Times Literary Supplement* (December 25, 1981), 1506. See n. 43 below.

42. S. A. Geller, *Parallelism in Early Biblical Poetry* (Missoula, Mont.: Scholars Press, 1979).

43. J. Kugel, *The Idea of Biblical Poetry* (New Haven, Conn.: Yale Univ. Press, 1981).

44. M. O'Connor, *Hebrew Verse Structure* (Winona Lake, Ind.: Eisenbrauns, 1980).

particular mode of expression of each psalm takes precedence over its place as a typical example of a genre. The concern is for the medium as well as the message, and the claim is that form and content cannot be separated. One is led to appreciate any psalm as a unique literary expression that unfolds its word in various traditional poetic devices and features. Interpreters who have moved in this direction have given particular attention to formal features of structure and the figures of speech that create structure, such as repetition, chiasmus, inclusion, word play, and ambiguity.[45]

Such stylistic analysis belongs to the study and understanding of any poetic text. It is consistent with larger trends in contemporary biblical study toward a primary focus on the final form of a text. It remains to be seen how well those whose sensitivity is to formal and poetic features will be able to place their work in the service of hermeneutics. To date, stylistic analysis often stands by itself without engaging other issues of interpretation.[46] But it is also the case that interpreters of the psalms whose attention is particularly given over to form-critical exegesis or to theological, liturgical, and pastoral dimensions of interpretation, have tended on the whole to ignore stylistic aspects as features of the text's expression. No modern commentary in English reflects any serious concentration on matters of style.[47] The full hearing of the psalms will be greatly enhanced when the familiar tendency to abstract content from form or to empty form of its content is overcome. To know the psalms are poetic is not to forget that they are Scripture. To read and hear them as Scripture requires that one receive them also as poetry. From either direction, *understanding* is all (see chap. 3).

---

45. Some representative examples of rhetorical or stylistic analysis of the psalms are N. J. Ridderbos, *Die Psalmen—Stilistischen Verfahren und Aufbau* (Berlin: Walter de Gruyter, 1972); M. Weiss, "Wege der neuen Dichtungswissenschaft in ihrer Anwendung auf die Psalmenforschung," *Biblica* 42 (1961): 255–302; L. Alonso-Schökel, *Treinta Salmos: Poesia y Oracion* (Madrid: Ediciones Christiandad, 1981); J. Trublet and J.-N. Aletti, *Approche poétique et théologique des psaumes* (Paris: Editions du Cerf, 1983); and P. Auffret, *La sagesse.*

46. Some of the works cited above are refreshing exceptions in this regard.

47. It is worth noting that the great form critic Hermann Gunkel gave major attention to the aesthetic features of the psalms in his commentary. See no. 1 above.

2. INTERPRETING THE PSALMS: SOME CLUES FROM THEIR HISTORY AND CONTENT

The interpreter of the psalms who takes them up to find afresh their lively meaning for contemporary faith does so with some advantages that are not necessarily present when other parts of the Old Testament are in view. The primary one is their general *familiarity*. Surely members of the community of faith know the psalms as well as or better than any part of Scripture, with the possible exception of the Gospels. That does not mean the familiarity is detailed, total, or highly informed. Indeed some of the psalms are quite unfamiliar and startling to persons when they first read them. All of us, however—even those on the outer fringes of religious involvement and commitment—have encountered the psalms sufficiently to feel their pulse, experience some of their vibrations, and know places within the Psalter that have some special meaning and importance for us as well as for others. Even persons who have little knowledge of the Old Testament or feel uncomfortable within its borders may feel at least somewhat at home with the psalms.

One of the most popular forms of publishing part of the Scriptures is the pocket New Testament with the Book of Psalms at the back. One can raise some questions about such an abbreviated collection of Scriptures that includes one testament and only one book out of the Old Testament, but I think appending the Psalter to the New Testament is a more positive and natural act than such questions about partiality and incompleteness would suggest. Placing the psalms after the New Testament arises out of the recognition that they in some sense provide a vehicle for responding to the good news of the loving and gracious activity of God that is proclaimed in the gospel. And here we come upon one of the significant characteristics of the psalms, one that poses issues for their interpretation but also rich possibilities. That is the fact that in the Psalter we have a large collection of words uttered to God and about God, but not by or from God. In other words the psalms give speech to human response and human existence before God (*coram Deo*). Furthermore life before God and in response to God is fully open and unrestricted. So it is that the psalms range through the gamut of *experiences* (disaster, war, sickness, exile, celebration, marriage, birth, death) and *emotions* (joy, terror, reflections, gratitude, hate, contentment, depression).

John Calvin in his commentary on the psalms articulates well the openness of these songs to the range of human emotions:

> I have been accustomed to call this, I think not inappropriately, "An Anatomy of All Parts of the Soul"; for there is not an emotion of which anyone can be conscious that is not here represented as in a mirror. Or rather, the Holy Spirit has here drawn to the life all the griefs, sorrows, fears, doubts, hopes, cares, perplexities, in short, all the distracting emotions with which the minds of men are wont to be agitated. The other parts of Scripture contain the commandments which God enjoined his servants to announce to us. But here the prophets themselves, seeing they are exhibited to us as speaking to God, and laying open all their inmost thoughts and affections, call, or rather draw, each of us to the examination of himself in particular, in order that none of the many infirmities to which we are subject, and the many vices with which we abound, may remain concealed.[1]

In similar fashion, but more succinctly, Martin Luther wrote:

> Where does one find finer words of joy than in the psalms of praise and thanksgiving? There you look into the hearts of all saints, as into fair and pleasant gardens, yes, as into heaven itself. There you see what fine and pleasant flowers of the heart spring up from all sorts of fair and happy thoughts toward God, because of his blessings. On the other hand, where do you find deeper, more sorrowful, more pitiful words of sadness than in the psalms of lamentation? There again you look into the hearts of all the saints, as into death, yes, as into hell itself. How gloomy and dark it is there, with all kinds of troubled forebodings about the wrath of God! So, too, when they speak of fear and hope, they use such words that no painter could so depict for you fear or hope, and no Cicero or other orator so portray them.
>
> And that they speak these words to God and with God, this, I repeat, is the best thing of all. This gives the words double earnestness and life. . . . Hence it is that the Psalter is the book of all saints; and everyone, in whatever situation he may be, finds in that situation psalms and words that fit

---

1. John Calvin, *Calvin's Commentaries* (Edinburgh: Calvin Translation Society, 1847), 1: xxxviii.

his case, that suit him as if they were put there just for his sake, so that he could not put it better himself, or find or wish for anything better.[2]

Calvin and Luther meant what they said, and they show various ways in which the psalms mirrored experiences and emotions of their own life and times. For Calvin, David's experiences and words in the psalms were analogous to his own and provided expression for his own response to God. So it has been for countless numbers who have read and prayed the psalms.

The psalms have also *functioned* in the community of faith in various ways. Walter Brueggemann aptly describes these functions:

> The hold that the Psalms have on the contemporary practice of faith and piety . . . is evident *liturgically* with regular and sustained use of the Psalms in the daily office, generation after generation. It is evident *devotionally* in those free church traditions which are not so keen on liturgic use but which nurture persons in their own prayer life to draw guidance and strength from the Psalms. And thirdly, contemporary use is evident *pastorally*, for many pastors find in the Psalms the most remarkable and reliable resources for many situations, for which the hospital call is paradigmatic. Thus, liturgical, devotional and pastoral uses are dimensions of the contemporary function of the Psalms.[3]

One may add to this analysis a fourth function that is the point of emphasis in this book: the *theological-homiletical* use of the psalms. This function, however, is fed by and grows out of the uses of the Psalter that Brueggemann identifies. The liturgical use of the psalms reminds us of a point I will elaborate at more length below, and that is that the psalms have functioned in the *worship* of the community of faith, Jewish and Christian, widely, extensively, and without break. Psalms have been read and sung in cycle in some denominations. Psalms have been turned into metrical hymns in other denominations. The community as a whole has prayed to God, praised God, and confessed its faith as it has sung and recited the Psalter. This means that there is a familiarity with, a customary use of, the Psalter in worship that opens the door for the congregation's listening to the exposition and interpretation of the meaning of the psalms, that provides a readiness to have their faith, their theology, their understanding of God informed by the very words they read, pray, confess, and sing. The *devotional* usage of the Psalter in-

---

2. Martin Luther, *Luther's Works*, vol. 35: *Word and Sacrament I* (Philadelphia: Fortress Press, 1960), 255–56.

3. Walter Brueggemann, "Psalms and the Life of Faith: A Suggested Typology of Function," *Journal for the Study of the Old Testament* 17 (1980):4–5.

dicates the way in which the psalms have been helpful, and especially the way in which they have been helpful to *individuals* in various facets of their personal experience. The place of the psalms in personal piety arises out of their capacity to express the character of the individual's relationship to God, especially aspects of devotion to God, such as trust, hope, assurance, but also some of the weariness, anxiety, and despair that come into our lives. Here is a kind of unreflective but authentic appropriation of the psalms that may function primarily at an emotional level, as it did for me not long ago when, in a conversation, my mother alluded to the verse in Psalm 103, "Like as a father pities his children so the Lord pities those who fear Him," and began weeping. She said, even as she cried, "I don't know why I am crying." That did not mean that she did not understand the words of the psalm. She is bright and theologically knowledgeable. But the impact of that verse was the impact of a lifetime of finding assurance and security in the basic conviction expressed there. It is no accident that Psalm 103 was read at my father's funeral, as it has been at many other such occasions. Such sense of the helpfulness of the psalms, such emotional response to the psalms, means once again a receptivity that allows the interpreter to explore even more deeply into the grounds and possibilities for these words of Scripture to be helpful, hopeful, and confirming.

The pastoral use of the psalms represents a similar feeling and conviction about the psalms. Here one is aware of the way in which the psalms give expression to anguish and offer themselves as prayers for those in extreme situations in crisis, sickness, death, and grief. A number of pastors have told me of the significant place that reading the psalms takes in their hospital ministry and their pastoral counseling. They give voice to the furthest corners of the human heart and offer words of comfort and healing to the deepest wounds, light to those who walk in shadow.

All of these functions help create the possibility that in the teaching and preaching enterprise the psalms may inform the faith and life of the congregation. It is to that end that these pages are written. I want to begin and, in a sense, to introduce the psalms for their theological and homiletical place by looking at how and why the psalms open themselves so readily and in so many ways for our appropriation, speaking both *for* us as they express our thoughts and feelings, fears and hopes, and *to* us as we hear in them direction for the life of faith and something of God's way with us.

One of the continuing problems that the interpreter of Scripture encounters is the sense of distance between our world and the world of

Scripture, the degree to which the text from Scripture comes from an ancient world that seems very remote from us and in many respects quite different. Narratives and stories of patriarchs and judges, kings and prophets, are very interesting and in various ways illuminating, but they often seem fairly remote from our experience. And it is the case for many persons that the better one understands these words of Scripture in and out of their *original* context, the more difficult it may be to hear their relevance and meaning to us in *our* context. I would argue, however, that the Psalter of the Old Testament bridges that gap between then and now, the ancient world and the present world, probably better than any other book of the Bible. There are several reasons for this.

The psalms are by their *history* not time-bound. Here, of course, is an important clue from the liturgical use of the psalms. They have never ceased to be the song book of Jewish and Christian communities. There is, therefore, an unbroken continuity that ties the ancient text to the present. There is nothing that the Christian interpreter *has* to do to place the psalms in the hands of his or her congregation. That congregation has carried this song book under its arm throughout all the centuries of its worship. This also means that the psalms are not simply an esoteric text. The bridge between past and present here is one of active use and personal involvement with and appropriation of the Psalter. The psalms have not been simply read as Scripture from the past but have been sung as words in and for the present. They have, therefore, a continuity in time, but they are not time-bound. When the congregation joins in the "we" of the psalms in such a statement as "God has blessed us; let all the ends of the earth fear God" it does not have to ask about some past story of God's blessing with Israel, but it claims in that moment the blessing of God and issues the call for all the peoples of this earth to praise and fear God.

The reality of the continuing existence of the psalms of the Old Testament as the church's hymn book goes a long way toward eliminating the need for special hermeneutical moves to make an ancient word and an Old Testament word relate to the contemporary congregation. It is not merely, if at all, an ancient word or an Old Testament word. The psalms have transcended and moved beyond either status as they have continued to be the community song book.

The psalms are by their *content* not time-bound. Apart from the superscriptions, the psalms are, along with the wisdom literature, the one large block of biblical literature that is not related to any particular period in Israel's history. There are historical references to the past, and there are clues that suggest a historical setting for some psalms. But even the most apparently obvious of such psalms remain to some degree debatable (e.g., Psalm 137). The elusiveness of the historical background of the psalms is further indicated by the unceasing debate about their dating and the widely contrasting views about that, which place the psalms from David and before on down to the Maccabean period. They are not easily placed in a particular period, both because historical clues are absent and because they can so easily be set in many different times and places as far as their content and character are concerned. The stories of Joshua are rooted in color and content in the beginnings of the nation Israel. Many of the prophets have a universal message, but that is properly cloaked in a particular setting and related to a particular prophet. The looseness of the psalms from all that historical rootage is not a problem but a gain and opens up interpretive possibilities.

Except in their superscriptions, on which see below, the psalms are not related to a specific person although they are highly and deeply personal. They are not bound to the experiences of one individual and her or his personal history. They are by definition *typical*, universal. They were composed, sung, prayed, collected, passed on because they have the capacity to articulate and express the words, thoughts, prayers of *anyone*, though they do not *necessarily* do that. They speak to and for typical human situations and thus have the capacity to speak to and for us as typical human beings. They have to do with experiences of *human* existence, not just Israel's existence or that of one human being. Let me illustrate by noting some of those expressions or images that reflect typical human experiences.

A very fundamental one, in my opinion, would be the image and the cry one finds at the beginning of Psalm 130:

> Out of the depths I cry to thee, O Lord!

The image of the depths and the crying out of the depths is not uncommon in the psalms. One finds it in the affirmation of Ps. 40:2:

> He drew me up from the desolate pit.

There is the related imagery of drowning, such as in the beginning of Psalm 69, or Ps. 42:7, or the combination of the imagery and experience of being in the depths and drowning under an overwhelming flood that one finds in the lament of Ps. 88:6–7. Both these images, the one of being thrust down or caught in the pit (see chap. 4) or down in the depths, or of being drowned in a flood that comes over one's head so that one cannot rise out of it, share the commonality of being the psalmic expressions of the experience of hopelessness and anxiety, of deep depression and a sense of being so overwhelmed by one's circumstances that there is no way out. One is so far down there is no way to get up. One is drowning and cannot overcome the floods. The pit of the Old Testament is equivalent to the contemporary expression I hear from time to time, "It's the pits!" When something is the pits, it is so bad it is hopeless. That experience rings through the psalms, and there is a core of imagery—one could add to it the experience of darkness and the affirmations of light that comes from the Lord—that gives full and vivid expression to this human experience, indeed, makes a point of contact with what many of us experience, far more than any psychological analysis could ever do.

Other images and typical experiences may be mentioned much more briefly:

(a) the frequent sense in the psalms of the transiency of human life (e.g., in Ps. 103:15 and Ps. 90:10);

(b) the experience that so many have had, incomplete but real, of the declaration of the glory of God in God's creation (e.g., in Psalms 8 and 19);

(c) the experience of God-forsakenness, the absence of God, the silence of God (e.g., in Pss. 9; 13:1; 19:1; 22:1–2; 83:1; see the exposition of Psalms 14 and 22 in Part 2); and on the other side of that,

(d) the fundamental experience of the trustworthiness of God, to which the popularity of the twenty-third Psalm is undoubtedly due (see the exposition of Psalm 23 in Part 2; even the imagery at the very beginning of the psalm, "The Lord is my shepherd," has a potency that outruns the experience most people have with shepherding: indeed, here is an example of the capacity of an image from an ancient time to catch hold and express powerfully a relationship, even when the image itself does not belong in a significant way to the common experience of contemporary persons);

(e) the sense of the joy and blessing of having children (e.g., in Psalms 127 and 128);

(f) the overwhelming sense of sin that one encounters in such a confession as Ps. 51:3: "I know my transgressions, my sin is ever before me";

(g) the universal experience of reaching for that which transcends ourselves, for the God who calls us into being and rules our lives, which is never more beautifully articulated than at the beginning of Psalm 42: "As a hart longs for flowing streams, so longs my soul for thee, O God. My soul thirsts for God, for the living God";

(h) the experience of the anxiety and despair of a human being who feels caught, trapped, hemmed in, an anguish expressed over and over again in the psalms through the imagery of being caught in a *net* (Ps. 10:9), being surrounded by inimical forces (Pss. 22:12 and 16) with terror on every side (Ps. 31:13), or being besieged by overwhelming forces (Ps. 31:21); and to articulate the positive side of this,

(i) the experience of God's help, of being given elbow room, a broad place where the petitioner is no longer trapped in, hemmed in, surrounded, and caught, but is free, has space, has room to be his or her own person (e.g., in Pss. 4:1; 18:19; 36; 31:8; 55:12; 118:5; 119:45); and finally,

(j) the experience of terribly low self-esteem and the sense of worthlessness we encounter in ourselves and in others that is brought to expression in the language of the great Psalm 22: "I am a worm, and not a person" (v. 6; my trans.).

Particular notice should be taken of all the expressions and images that have to do with sickness. The laments and complaints about sickness and their prayers for healing have possibilities for our contemporary appropriation. They provide the words to help us pray for and think about sickness and health.

There has been much scholarly discussion about sickness in the psalms, what it is, how literally one should understand the allusions to illness, what the cultic setting was in which prayers for healing or complaints about sickness were uttered. All of that, however, may be beside the point. Sickness is a situation of extremity, a situation of utter disorientation: everything comes apart; one no longer feels in control; one feels caught; the very body dissolves before us. In situations of deep sickness and pain one is so controlled and dominated and undone by the illness that it is almost impossible to think about or deal with any other aspect of life. Nearly everyone has experienced a sickness—even if only briefly—when he or she feels about to die, even wants to die. One may not actually be on the edge of death but feels that way. I have never been on the edge of death; I have felt like death and even wanted to die in sickness. Whether the descriptions of sickness and illness in the psalms are to be taken literally or not is irrelevant. They may describe at

times an actual sickness or speak to or for a person *now* in sickness. Or
the poet may be using imagery, and the contemporary reader may appropriate it as powerful image of distress. The language of "bones languishing," heart throbbing, strength failing (for example, in Psalm 38) is
vivid and familiar to anyone's experience (see the exposition of Psalm 22
in Part 2). One feels helpless, oppressed by forces outside oneself—and
indeed that is the situation. Moaning, groaning, sighing, tears, the experience, Why is this happening to me?—all are aspects of the distress
of sickness.

   **There are also some places and ways in which the psalms do seem
time-bound by history and content.** But if one listens a little longer, one
can again find openings for hearing the psalms as songs and prayers
that do not sound foreign to us even when placed on our very contemporary lips.

   Some historicizing of the psalms has taken place, for example, in the
superscriptions where the psalms are often related to a famous person
or persons, and not infrequently a specific event. The most common superscription, of course, is the title "A Psalm of David," which is given to
so many of the particular psalms. In several of the psalms, particularly
Psalms 51—60, there is a reference to some event in the life of David, for
example, in Psalm 60, "A Miktam of David; for instruction; when he
strove with Aram-naharaim and with Aram-zobah, and when Joab on
his return killed twelve thousand of Edom in the Valley of Salt." These
psalm superscriptions are usually ignored on several grounds. The most
legitimate reason for doing so is that we do not understand some of
them or what they refer to. But these obscurities are usually found in the
technical musical references in the psalm titles. The historical references
are much clearer and easier to understand. These are commonly ignored
on two grounds: *(a)* they are later additions to the text; and *(b)* they do
not give accurate historical information. That dismissal of the superscriptions is much too facile, however, for they can serve a hermeneutical or interpretive purpose. They are not merely historical footnotes
about authorship whose value is dependent entirely on their reliability.
In two ways they open up possibilities for interpretation: (1) They suggest a circumstance in which the introduced psalm would be appropriate and thus provide an illustrative clue to interpretation (see chap. 4).
(2) The ascription of psalms to David is not simply to give an author's
identity but to receive them from the lips and heart of one who in many
respects was as much a representative human being as any figure in the

Old Testament. For David clearly was that. He was the human creature in his sin and weakness, exemplified most clearly in the Bathsheba and Uriah episode. He was the human being in his anguish and despair as exemplified most clearly in the Absalom episode, but he also was the one who embodied and represented the rule of God. He was the one upon whom the judgment was given that he was a man after God's own heart. Now it is that sort of ambiguous mixture of good and bad, joy and despair, obedience and disobedience, that is what we all are. So when these psalms are given to us from the lips of David, they are given to us from one who lived and felt and responded as one of us, whose hatred could run deep, whose agony could be unbearable, who cried out to God in confidence that he had tried to serve God faithfully, and who could fear the judgment of God because of the terrible weight of his own sinfulness. In the psalms of David we see our own image, our own profile, and indeed, in one of the psalms (Psalm 102), which is like so many of the psalms of David that it could have been listed as one of them, the superscription says that it belongs to an anonymous afflicted one, faint and pouring out complaint before the Lord—someone like David, like me, who is undone and pours out his or her heart in anguish, and indeed anger and complaint, before the Lord.

The psalms have a rich interaction with the New Testament. A sense of the place of the psalms in faith and life, as well as further interpretive clues to their understanding, may be found in the fact that the psalms have a rich interaction with the New Testament. The New Testament draws more heavily on the Psalms than on any other book of the Old Testament. Psalm 22, for example, provides the fundamental interpretive key to the Passion of Jesus (see the exposition of Psalm 22 in Part 2). What is clear as one reads the psalms is that they are promissory. They have an anticipatory character that presses them forward toward the New Testament. Note how much the psalms speak of (a) salvation coming; (b) waiting for the Lord and the Lord's deliverance (e.g., 25:5, 21; 27:14; 31:24; 38:15; 40:1); and (c) God's light (e.g., 43:3). This last reference,

> Oh send out thy light and thy truth;
> let them lead me, (43:3)

resonates with the New Testament's identification of Jesus with the light (John 12:35–36, 46) and the truth (John 14:6).

The psalms also speak of leading us in the way, and we hear in this the New Testament word that identifies Jesus with the way (see the exposition of Psalm 1 in Part 2). They also speak of the Lord as Shepherd (23:1; 28:9), which resonates with Jesus' self-declaration, "I am the good shepherd" who gives life and gives it abundantly (John 10:11; see the exposition of Psalm 23 in Part 2).

In Matthew 21:9 and parallels, the crowds greet Jesus' entry into Jerusalem with the words of Psalm 118:25–26: "Hosannah, blessed is he that comes in the name of the Lord." And the cry "Hosannah" is partly a greeting, but it is also the basic petition of the psalms, "Save us, Lord." In that cry the psalms and Jesus meet, as all those cries that run throughout the psalms and had been sung for centuries, "Save us, Lord/save me, Lord," are now addressed to the one who has come to save.

The psalms refer to the Lord's anointed (e.g., Psalm 2), and this was heard by the Christian community as meaning not primarily past kings or even unknown kings but *the* anointed, *Ho Christos,* the Christ, Jesus of Nazareth (see the exposition of Psalm 2 in Part 2). Further, the psalmists pray for, hope, anticipate, expect the Lord's deliverance of them from the threat of death, and through the New Testament all these utterances gain a deeper and fuller meaning. We listen to them now, at least in part, in the knowledge of the victory of God and the resurrection of Jesus Christ (see the exposition of Psalm 14 in Part 2).

What happens, therefore, as we read the psalms with the New Testament is that they interact with one another, they talk to one another. The Psalms draw us to Jesus, make us think of him; they gain their specificity, their reality for us, their concreteness, in the revelation of Jesus. But it is the case, also, that that interaction works the other way, and our thinking and interpretation and our preaching about Jesus of Nazareth needs to be conversation with the psalms, for the psalms provide some of the fundamental content for what the reality of Jesus is as salvation, light, hope, deliverance, shepherd.

To comprehend what those images are as they come to fulfillment in Jesus requires that we hear the words of those who hope and anticipate, that we listen carefully to their cries and prayers, for it is surely the case that to the extent that Jesus is the answer, one must have heard what the questions are. And in that sense, the questions, the hopes, the needs to which Jesus is the divine response, the answer of God, are found on the lips of the psalmists, and thus on our lips as we sing the psalms.

3. POETRY AND INTERPRETATION

The Psalms are poetry. They are rhythmic and expressive. They walk around a thought, say it one way here, another there. They create climaxes in a very few lines. All of these things are things a poem does. Horace, in his *Art of Poetry*, declared that the aim of a poet is either to instruct or to delight a reader, or preferably to do both. There is a long critical discussion, reaching all the way back to Aristotle at least and continuing down to the present in varying degrees of intensity, about whether or not one of those purposes should have priority over the other or whether one of them is in fact invalid or of little importance. Babette Deutsch has defined poetry as "the art which uses words as both speech and song to reveal the realities that the senses record, the feelings salute, the mind perceives, and the shaping imagination orders."[1] All of that points the reader to three basic qualities of poetry: *(a)* a particular *content*, *(b)* a particular *form*, and *(c)* a particular *effect*. The last is what Horace had in mind; that is, the result of a poem. But that result is achieved by content, and in a poem the content involves emotion, imagination, and meaning, and is marked by power and beauty. It is conveyed in a form—for example, verse, rhyme, strophe, meter, and the like.

Those of us who read, hear, say, or interpret the psalms in the context of the church probably sense and resonate to poetic dimensions but in a way that remains for the most part at a surface level. Or, to put it differently, we tend to come down on one side of the possible aims that

1. C. Hugh, *A Handbook to Literature* (Indianapolis: Bobbs-Merrill, 1972), 405.

Horace and others have identified. When we come to the Scriptures our primary concern is semantic and not aesthetic; that is, we are interested in meaning rather than beauty. Attention to aesthetic dimensions of biblical poetry is a little suspect. Scripture is meant to edify. Other purposes or results, other effects on us, are less important, if not irrelevant. But such an approach is to ignore the very nature of poetry, as Deutsch and other poets and critics have well perceived. Meaning and beauty, the semantic and the aesthetic, are woven together into a whole, and both should be received and responded to by the interpreter. To ignore the beauty in pursuit of the meaning is, at a minimum, to close out the possibility that the beauty in a significant fashion contributes to and enhances the meaning. To illustrate, I may have as my goal to transport myself from one city to another. In carrying out that enterprise I can ignore the vehicle that gets me there and the route; but while the means and the way may not be the primary concern, the size and condition of the vehicle and the scenic character of the route can affect when I get there and my physical and psychic condition when I arrive. For biblical poetry, if not for literature generally, Marshall McLuhan was at least partially correct with his famous dictum "The medium is the message." The medium or vehicle of poetry and the message of the text are thoroughly interrelated.

This means that poetry and interpretation are not matters that should be dealt with separately; rather, a deeper sensitivity to the poetic character of the text can enhance our understanding, and attention to poetic features may aid the interpretive process and its results. Even more, they may do much of the task of enabling us to appropriate the word of the psalm or the biblical poem as our own. In the pages that follow I would like to illustrate how attention to poetic features may contribute to understanding and appropriating the biblical psalms.

PARALLELISM

One of the primary characteristics of biblical poetry, as indeed of poetry generally, is a sense of balance between or among the elements that make up the poetry. One element in various ways matches or balances another element. Or several components of a poem may match or balance one another. In biblical poetry this balance is traditionally understood to be manifest in three ways: rhythm, length, and meaning. Balance in rhythm is commonly expressed under the rubric of meter, two halves of a line of poetry having roughly the same number of accented syllables. Various analyses of the meter of biblical poetry have been set forth, no one of which has gained a general consensus of support. Part of the problem is the absence of the kind of regularity that one is accustomed to in classical meter. Indeed, some have argued for the complete absence of meter in Hebrew poetry or, more accurately, for the view that what is perceived as meter, that is, rhythmic balance, arises out of the presence of parallelism. Balance in length has to do with the number of syllables in a half line or colon of poetry.[2] This too is a poetic criterion that is subject to varying approaches as well as skepticism about its viability. Some analyses of syllable counts follow the present or Masoretic vocalization of the Hebrew text. Others seek to restore an earlier pre-Masoretic vocalization.

For the interpreter of Scripture, the balance of lines in terms of rhythm and length is not only problematic but less useful as far as understanding and illumination of the text are concerned, though such balance does contribute to the perceived aesthetic experience of the text. The expression of balance in terms of *meaning*, however, is a phenomenon of the text that should be observed and can aid the interpreter in gaining a sensitive, nuanced, and full reading of the passage under consideration. This, of course, is true not only for the psalms but also for the many other songs, prophetic oracles, and proverbs that are set forth in poetic form.

Balance in meaning is set forth primarily in what is commonly known as *parallelism*, a term derived from the fact that elements within a line often seem to parallel or match each other, that is, that the subject in the first colon of a line is the subject in the second colon, though often expressed or identified with a different word. The verb of one colon often is similar to (or the opposite of) the verb of the other colon. To use the examples from Ps. 24:1–2 cited in n. 2 the subject of v. 2 is the same in

---

2. In this discussion we will use the word colon (plural = cola) for the two or more parts of a line that balance each other in some fashion. Verses contain one or more lines; most lines contain two or three cola. In the RSV a printed line usually equals a colon and the balancing second colon of the line will be slightly indented. Here is an example from Ps. 24:1–2:

line	{	The earth is the Lord's and the fullness thereof,	—colon
		the world and those who dwell therein;	—colon
		(v. 1)	
line	{	for he has founded it upon the seas,	—colon
		and established it upon the rivers.	—colon
		(v. 2)	

A line with two cola is a *bicolon*; three cola constitute a *tricolon*. In some discussions of poetry one will find the term stich or stichos for colon and distich or tristich for bicolon and tricolon, but this is a decreasingly common system of terminology.

both cola, the verbs "founded" and "established" are similar, the objects are the same, and the prepositional phrases "upon the seas" and "upon the rivers" balance each other. In v. 1 there is no parallel to the possessive reference to the Lord in the second colon, but "the world" and "the earth" parallel each other and "the fullness thereof" (or "its fullness") is balanced by "those who dwell therein."

The reader of the psalms or other biblical poetry is quickly struck by this characteristic, and it is indeed the most noticeable feature of those poems. The effort to describe this phenomenon satisfactorily, however, or to give it a conceptual analysis that would take account of all forms or manifestations of parallelism, has been difficult, though there have been many attempts. The chief problem is the existence of a large number of variations in the way the cola balance each other. Some are opposite, for example, Ps. 1:6:

> for the Lord knows the way of the righteous,
>   but the way of the wicked will perish.

The elements are by no means precisely parallel, but the sense of balance between "way of the righteous" and "way of the wicked," and between "the Lord knows" and "[it] will perish" is felt immediately by the reader or hearer. In other cases, the reader will sense no parallelism of meaning at all, as in Ps. 10:17–18, where v. 17 shows clear balance of meaning or parallelism, but v. 18 seems devoid of that altogether.

> v. 17: The desire of the weak you will hear, O Lord;
>   you will strengthen their heart,
>   you will make your ear attentive,
>
> v. 18: to do justice to the orphans and the oppressed
>   so that one who is of the earth may
>   never again strike terror.
>   (my trans.)

The traditional way of handling these differences is to classify verses of biblical poetry under three types of parallelism: synonymous (e.g., Ps. 24:1), antithetic (e.g., Ps. 1:6), and synthetic (e.g., Ps. 10:18). Recent studies, however, have tended to move away from this approach out of recognition of the fact that there are so many variations of these types that a three-category classification is misleading or so subject to various qualifications as to be of little use. Consequently, alternative analyses have developed that move in opposite directions, as I have indicated briefly in chapter 1. One approach is to describe and classify the many

variations so that one ends up with a large number of types of parallelism or poetic lines.[3] The other approach, which has been set forth most
fully and impressively by James Kugel,[4] is to see in parallelism an essentially single phenomenon that is expressed in many ways. Somewhere
in between, at least as far as categorizing parallel pairs of words and
phrases rather than whole cola, is the list of Stephen Geller,[5] which distinguishes between synonyms, lists, antonyms, merismus, epithets,
proper nouns, pronouns, metonyms, concrete-abstract, numbers, repetition, and metaphor. While it is not necessary to make a sharp choice
between these options, Kugel's way of describing the phenomenon of
parallelism is probably more useful and accessible to the interpreter
whose focus is more upon semantic—that is, meaning—dimensions
than upon grammatical or syntactical ones.

In this approach, biblical poetry is seen to have as its most characteristic feature the parallelistic line composed of two parts that can relate to
each other in many ways, all of which, however, assume that the second
part or colon (B) is connected to the first part or colon (A) and has something in common with it. The second part (B) of the line serves a seconding function, particularizing, defining, or expanding the meaning of
the first part (A). Kugel defines this relation as "A is so, and *what's more*,
B is so," indicating that the parallelism consists in the fact that "B typically *supports* A, carries it further, backs it up, completes it, goes beyond
it" (*The Idea of Biblical Poetry*, 52). The relation between the cola may be of
the character "since A, therefore B," "if A, then B," "A happened, and B
happened," and the like. What happens in these parallelistic lines and
thus what distinguishes biblical prose from biblical poetry is that the latter employs "a complex of heightening effects used in combinations and
intensities that vary widely from composition to composition" (p. 92).
The more elevated or heightened the style by such devices as parallelism, ellipsis, chiasmus, figures of speech, alliteration, or assonance, the
more the speech is poetic. The paralleling or seconding feature is the primary one.

Recognition of this parallelistic phenomenon and sensitivity to its
varying manifestations and their common character as expressing a

3. See Terence Collins, *Line Forms in Hebrew Poetry* (Rome: Pontifical Biblical Inst. Press,
1978), and Michael O'Connor, *Hebrew Verse Structure* (Winona Lake, Ind.: Eisenbrauns,
1980), both of which are analyses of the many syntactic variations of poetry rather than
analyses of types of strictly semantic parallels.
    4. James Kugel, *The Idea of Biblical Poetry* (New Haven, Conn.: Yale Univ. Press, 1981).
    5. Stephen Geller, *Parallelism in Early Biblical Poetry* (Chico, Calif.: Scholars Press, 1979),
34–41.

thought or idea in elevated style with the second expression seconding, emphasizing, or elaborating the first can give to the interpreter and communicator a grasp of the richness and power of the word being interpreted. The presence of the B or parallel colon serves to nuance the original or prior word of the A colon. It underscores it in some fashion or adds to our understanding some element that is not clearly indicated in the first colon. All of this when appropriated by the interpreter serves to enrich the language and concepts available for speaking about the meaning of the text. Some examples can illustrate this so that one may read the Psalms and begin to draw upon their poetic effect and intention as a part of the intentionality and communication of the text.

The first two verses of Psalm 24, cited as examples of parallelism above, demonstrate how the second colon reinforces the first in different ways. Verse 1:

    A   The earth is the Lord's and the fullness thereof,
    B   the world and those who dwell therein

The A colon has established the basic point that the whole earth and all it contains belong to the Lord. The B colon seconds that point but by particular *specification* within the fullness, that is, by mention of the inhabitants of the world of God's. The reader hears the general claim that everything on earth belongs to God and is then drawn to focus on the fact that this means that the people or inhabitants of the earth are God's. Verse 2:

    A   for he has founded it upon the seas,
    B   and established it upon the rivers.

Structurally this verse serves to give the reason or ground for the large claim made in v. 1. Within the poetic line, where in some sense every element in A is closely matched by a synonymous or nearly synonymous element in B, the second or B colon emphasizes the point of A by declaring that the rivers as well as the seas are the foundations of the divinely established order. The point is in effect repeated and underlined.

Psalm 2:2 shows the way in which successive cola second earlier ones by elaborating and expanding:

    A   The kings of the earth set themselves
    B   and the rulers take counsel together,
    C   against the Lord and his anointed.

While the second colon (B) is clearly parallel to the first (A), it does not merely repeat the thought of A but intensifies and elaborates it. The rulers not only take their stand, they counsel or conspire together. The verb in B explains in a quite specific way that goes beyond A. The third colon (C) is sometimes omitted by commentators as a gloss. There is no compelling reason for that, however. Again the colon moves on to intensify and elaborate in a startling way by identifying the object of the action of kings and rulers. That action is emphasized and explained by the double object in colon C. The tricolon as a whole serves to build in intensity as each successive colon adds a dimension to the basic thought in the first colon. The interpreter is led by the poetic process to hear the development of thought and the force of each new dimension as he or she hears the members of the poetic line. The conspiracy and the double object each are highlighted in the movement of the line.

The first verse of the Psalter (1:1) is a classic case of parallelism that exemplifies well the power of the seconding feature of biblical poetry:

> Blessed is the one who
>   walks not in the counsel of the wicked
>   nor stands in the way of sinners,
>   nor sits in the seat of scoffers.
>   (my trans.)

The first phrase, "Blessed is the one," stands outside the parallelism. The rest of the verse describes the one who is blessed in a series of obviously parallel cola that again emphasize and intensify the basic point, which is stated in the first of the parallel cola: the one who does not walk in the counsel of the wicked. The wicked are spoken of appropriately in the first colon, for they are the dominant category of those who go the wrong way in the Psalter generally and specifically in this Psalm (vv. 4–6). They are the ones who oppose God and the righteous or innocent at every point. But as the seconding cola indicate, the sinners also, that is, those whose acts or conduct are violations of the norms or rules of the community, are those from whom the righteous one separates himself or herself. What's more, and more specifically, the arrogant ones who scoff at others, insult them, and scorn them are also to be avoided. The cola thus move from the dominant category to more specific examples, each one in some way elaborating, underscoring, and broadening the reader's vision of those groups whose quality of life does not bring blessing.

In a similar way the other elements in the parallelism serve to emphasize and elaborate the point of the first of the three parallel cola. The negative response to the advice and counsel of the wicked is under-

scored and developed by balancing and paralleling it with rejection of
the mode of conduct or style of life and destiny, that is, the "way" of
sinners. And finally, association and comradeship with scoffers is set
aside by this wise and righteous one. The verbs serve also to emphasize
the point as they encompass primary modes of human action and involvement—going or walking; standing; and sitting. In one verse,
therefore, the richness of expression that is developed in the parallelism
conveys vividly, emphatically, and fully the total rejection on the part of
the righteous of everything having to do with the wicked and wickedness. The interpreter of the psalm is given a breadth of expression and
ideas for hearing and re-presenting the strong No! of the righteous one
that leads to or brings about blessing.

To take a whole psalm as an example, one can see a variety of ways in
which parallelism in the poetic lines of Psalm 29 conveys various dimensions of the communication. The first two verses of the psalm show the
seconding and emphasizing effect carrying not just from first colon to
second but from one line to the next:

A   Ascribe to the Lord, O heavenly beings,
B   ascribe to the Lord glory and strength.
                                             (v. 1)
A   Ascribe to the Lord the glory of his name;
B   worship the Lord in holy array.
                                             (v. 2)

In v. 1, the imperative is underscored by its repetition, which is followed
by yet a third call to ascribe to the Lord. The parallelism serves to show
with a high degree of intensity what the psalm is set to do, that is, call to
the praise of God. The second colon of v. 1 then elaborates the first one
by moving from the identification of those summoned to praise, that is,
the divine ones, to declare what it is about the Lord that is to be praised
or ascribed to him, that is, glory and might. Verse 2 picks up at that
point but again serves both to underscore and to elaborate by saying it is
glory that is ascribed, but that glory is identified and given its content
and specificity by being defined as the glory due to or appropriate to the
Lord's name, being, and character. The seconding colon then serves to
reinforce and explain as it indicates that this ascription to the Lord
means the worship and homage of God.

A   The voice of the Lord is upon the waters;
B   the God of glory thunders,
C   the Lord, upon many waters.
                                             (v. 3)

It is possible that the A and B cola were in reverse order in the original form of this poem, but even in the present order the shape of the poetic line bears the reader along as the B colon explains the meaning of the image of the voice of the Lord and the C colon emphasizes and intensifies the A colon by the simple addition of "many" to "waters." The B colon serves, therefore, to explain the imagery and the C colon to underscore and strengthen it.

A   The voice of the Lord is powerful,
B   the voice of the Lord is full of majesty.
                                        (v. 4)

Here not only does the B colon emphasize the point of the A colon, but the whole verse again serves that function in regard to v. 3. One hears now a second focus of the psalm arising out of the repetitions in parallel, that is, *the voice of God*.

A   The voice of the Lord breaks the cedars,
B   the Lord breaks the cedars of Lebanon.
                                        (v. 5)

The force of the imagery of the voice of the Lord as a mighty storm is carried from the storm upon the waters that stirs them up (v. 3) to the power of the storm of God that shatters the cedar trees. Then the parallel or B colon seconds the thought and picture of the A colon by specifying and thus sharpening the image. It is the great cedars of Lebanon, symbol of glory and strength, that are unable to withstand the force of the voice of the Lord in the storm. A similar specification occurs in v. 8, where "wilderness" is paralleled by "wilderness of Qadesh."

A   He makes Lebanon to skip like a calf,
B   and Sirion like a young wild ox.
                                        (v. 6)

The power of the divine storm is so terrifying and overwhelming that it makes mountains dance or skip about in fright (cf. Psalm 114). The point that is made in A (the Lebanon mountains skipping like a frightened calf) is emphasized by the comparison of Sirion to a wild ox in the same state.

A   The Lord sits enthroned over the flood;
B   the Lord sits enthroned as king for ever.
                                        (v. 10)

Verses 7–9 contain some serious problems for anyone trying to establish the poetic lines and so should not be used as examples in this context. But v. 10 shows the further use of a repetitive parallelism where the second colon (B) emphasizes the first and takes it a step further. The Lord's rule over chaotic flood or flood dragon is underscored as it is declared to be an eternal rule.

A   May the Lord give strength to his people!
B   May the Lord bless his people with peace!
(v. 11)

Not only does the Lord give might to the people; the Lord also blesses them with security, safety, peace. The parallel colon both seconds and expands the claim of the A colon so that the reader hears in stronger fashion and in further development the beneficence of God to the people.

The ways in which the psalmists used one colon to reinforce, elaborate, or second the other colon are illustrated well in those cases where the same colon in different contexts is balanced and seconded by varying B cola. One notes, for example, the different ways in which the A colon is matched in the following examples:

A   O sing to the Lord a new song;
B   sing to the Lord all the earth.
(96:1)

A   O sing to the Lord a new song,
B   for he has done marvelous things!
(98:1)

A   Sing to the Lord a new song,
B   his praise in the assembly of the faithful!
(149:1)

In one case (96:1), A is seconded in repetitive fashion that expands A by identifying those who are called to sing. In another instance (98:1), the seconding move is made in giving a reason for the command of the A colon. And finally (149:1), the emphasis is not on the command but on the what and where of the song.

One finds a similar typology of seconding cola for the same A colon in the following examples:

A   Turn to me and be gracious to me;
B   give thy strength to thy servant,
        and save the son of thy handmaid.
(86:16)

A Turn to me and be gracious to me;
B   for I am lonely and afflicted.
(25:16)

A Turn to me and be gracious to me,
B   as is thy wont toward those who
      love thy name.
(119:132)

In each case the command is seconded and followed up by a different B colon, one reiterating the command in different language, one giving a reason, and one reinforcing the command by rooting it in the character of God.

A very frequent effect of the paralleling or seconding of the line is more particular specifying of something that has been said more generally in the first colon; or vice versa, the reader is led to a generalizing from an already encountered particular example. Sometimes this is done by the use of synecdoche, the figure of thought whereby *the whole is represented by a part*, as when, for example, in the royal psalms the crown (Ps. 21:3) or the scepter (Ps. 110:2) is used to speak of the whole dominion of the king. A good example is found in Ps. 18:27:

A For you deliver a humble [*ānî*] people;
B   but the haughty eyes ['*ênayim*] you bring down.
(my trans.)

In the first colon (A) the general category, that is, people, is stated as the object of the Lord's activity. In the B colon that object is now set forth in a lively way by using a part, that is, people's eyes, to speak of the whole, the actual people themselves. The poetic and aesthetic dimension is elevated and the communication sharpened in the process. Two things seem to evoke the particularizing of the second colon. One is the creation of wordplay in the Hebrew in the form of *alliteration* and *assonance* as the word "eyes" echoes the sequence of letters '-n-y that one has already encountered in the word "humble," leading the reader to hear more sharply the juxtaposition and thus the real contrast between the humble who are delivered by God and the haughty who are brought low (note that in the English a similar effect is created by the initial sounds of the words "humble" and "haughty." The other reason for the B colon formulation is that raising the eyes is one of the ways that persons express haughtiness and pride. The effect of the poetry is to create a vivid image in the mind's eye of the type of persons God will bring down.

The move from the general to the specific and vice versa can happen poetically also by the *balance of concrete and abstract terms*, a fairly frequent poetic device illustrated again in Psalm 18, this time in v. 24:

A   Therefore, the Lord has recompensed me according to my
    righteousness,
B   according to the cleanness of my hands in his sight.

The general and abstract term "righteousness" is made more specific with the spelling out in the B colon of clean hands, itself a metaphorical way of speaking about and imagining moral conduct. In Ps. 91:5–6 the abstract notion of terror is made concrete in the second colon with the reference to a weapon, arrows:

A   You will not fear the terror of the night,
B   nor the arrow that flies by day,
                              (v. 5)

A   nor the pestilence that stalks in darkness,
B   nor the destruction that wastes at noonday.
                              (v. 6)

These two verses also each manifest *merismus*, a figure of thought wherein two polar or opposite terms are placed in parallel so that together they convey the notion of *totality*. That happens in these verses in the polarities of "night" and "day" and "darkness" and "noonday." The double merismus conveys to any reader the psalmist's strong sense that under any and every circumstance God will provide protection.

One of the most common features of literary style in both prose and poetry is *repetition*. The very fact of repetition may tend to dull us into overlooking it when its presence is meant to have the opposite effect, that is, to catch our attention. It may occur in various ways and for different purposes. One of the forms of repetition in the psalms is what is called *inclusion*. Here an element, colon, or line at the beginning of a text or part of a text is repeated at the end of the unit, to recall the beginning and in so doing underscore the initial word of the psalm. This is especially common in psalms of praise, which often, if not usually, open in a call to praise. Inasmuch as eliciting praise of God is the primary purpose of such psalms, it is appropriate to sound that note again as the final word. One sees this, for example, in the repetition of "Hallelujah," "Praise the Lord," in Psalms 106, 113, 117, and 146—150, and in the beginnings and endings of Psalms 8, 118, and 136, where the basic intention of the psalm is expressed in the opening verse, and the singers or readers are then brought back to declare and hear that point again. A similar thing happens in Psalms 103 and 104, where the fundamental aim to give thanks and praise is never lost because it is both the beginning and ending word ("Bless the Lord, O my soul") and in Psalm 103 is repeated several times ("Bless the Lord") at the beginning and end.

Repetition of words or phrases or lines can also serve a structural function to give the reader clues about how to hold things together and how to mark off sections and units of thought from one another in the movement of the psalm. The "Blessed . . ." at the beginning of Psalm 1 and the end of Psalm 2 is an inclusion that indicates these two psalms in some way are to be held or read together (see the expositions of these psalms in Part 2). Although it is not strictly an inclusion, in the sense that the first occurrence is not right at the beginning, the repetition of "there is none that does good" in vv. 1 and 3 of Psalm 14 helps the reader see those verses as a section of the psalm and the repeated "there is none . . ." set alongside the "there is no God" causes the reader to hear those two expressions together and ask if there is any relationship (see the exposition of Psalm 14 in Part 2).

Such repetitions of cola or whole lines to mark off units of thought may occur several times within a poem as a kind of refrain to mark stanzas as, for example, the frequently repeated "for his steadfast love endures forever" in Psalm 136 or the threefold repetition in Psalms 42—43 of the refrain,

> Why are you cast down, O my soul,
>   and why are you disquieted within me?
> Hope in God; for I shall again praise him,
>   my help and my God.

This repetition accomplishes three purposes, which the interpreter can readily see. It leads one to see Psalm 43 as in some fashion a continuation of Psalm 42, so that the two psalms need to be read together. It marks off the main thought units of these psalms. Perhaps most important of all, this repetition represents one of the primary movements of thought in the psalms, a kind of repeated mood change. For in each of the three sections marked off by this refrain the psalmist expresses distress and despair and a sense of God's abandonment. The repeated refrain each time serves in a sense to call the psalmist back on track, remembering that hope is in God who will yet deliver. In each section, therefore, the psalmist goes down but comes back up via the dialogue with the soul or the self.

In that repetition in Psalms 42—43, the theme or point is underscored while the sections of the psalms are set off. The same is true with the refrain in vv. 7 and 11 of Psalm 46:

> The Lord of hosts is with us,
>   the God of Jacob is our refuge.

The whole point of the psalm is wrapped up in that line, which also echoes the beginning verse. Another kind of poetic repetition occurs here, which we have noted in passing elsewhere. That is the repeated use of particular words, which causes the reader to place in some juxtaposition to each other the contexts in which those words occur. Frequently, as is the case here, the repetition of a single word is not discernible in the translation, where different English words may be used. Here is where access to the Hebrew is useful, though frequently a good commentary will point out such repetitions, and it is then the task of the interpreter to appropriate them and reflect on their role in the text's communication. Psalm 46 envisages the possible chaotic breakdown of the natural world (vv. 1–3) and the nations (vv. 4–7)—all of which is caught up in the several references to "earth"—and declares the sure refuge of God in the midst of the worst tumult imaginable (vv. 8–10). One of the ways that basic point is scored is in the three uses of the verb *mût*, meaning "to shake, totter" (Heb.=vv. 3, 6, and 7; Eng.=vv. 2, 5, and 6). In the first case it refers to the mountains shaking (*mût*) in the heart of the sea; in the third case it refers to the nations and kingdoms tottering (*mût*). But in between those two uses of the verb to describe a kind of return to total chaos, the poet uses the same verb with a negative to say that the city wherein God is present shall not shake or totter ("she shall *not be moved*," v. 5). With a special clarity achieved by this verbal repetition the reader is led to contrast the fate of the kingdoms of the earth and the natural world over against the unshakable security of that community in which God truly dwells.

A similar use of repetition occurs in Psalm 6, where the verb *bāhal*, "to trouble, terrify," occurs in vv. 2–3 to describe the plight of the lamenting psalmist (". . . my bones are troubled. My soul also is sorely troubled," vv. 2–3) and then is used by the psalmist as a part of the plea to God to the effect that the same thing should be the fate of the workers of evil who in some fashion have oppressed the psalmist (v. 10a). Thus a kind of irony or poetic justice is sounded in the psalm.

Repetition with the effect of creating irony occurs elsewhere, for example, in the use of the verb *šûb*, "to turn, return," in Psalm 90. It occurs twice in v. 3:

You *turn* humankind back to the dust,
    and say, *"Turn back*, O mortal ones!"
                (my trans.)

The word "turn" means at one level a return to the dust from which human life comes (Gen. 3:19). But the second use is ambiguous and in some sense ironic, for the expression "turn back" can mean God's command that sends mortals to their final state, dust, or it can mean God's call to mortals to repent—another meaning of *šûb* in Hebrew and one that is fully consonant with the psalm's emphasis upon humanity's limited life span and consequent return to the earth's being tied in to God's judgment for sins. A third use of *šûb* in v. 13 serves as the psalmist's call to *God* to turn! In this case the verb refers to God's turning back in grace and mercy to those from whom God has earlier turned away.

A final example of repetition creating a juxtaposition or sharp contrast in the mind of the reader is readily observable in the use of the word "hand" in Psalm 31. Twice a contrast is set up between the hand of God, which is an image of protection and reassurance, and the hand of the enemy, which is an image of threat:

Into *your hand* I commit my spirit
                (v. 5)

You have not delivered me *into the*
    hand of the enemy
                (v. 8)

and:

My times are *in your hand;*
deliver me *from the hand of my*
enemies and persecutors.
                (v. 15; my trans.)

The above discussion suggests the possible effects and purposes, and gives examples, of one of the primary rhetorical features of poetry—that is, repetition (many of the same effects are created by the use of repetition in prose, but that is not under discussion here). Another poetic feature that contributes to the interpreter's appropriation of the text as it is seen and studied is *ambiguity*. Where ambiguity is perceived in the text, it may not be a problem of understanding, that is, of trying to find the "correct" meaning out of the possibilities discerned, but rather may be a pointer to the richness of a text where dual or multiple meanings may truly present themselves to the reader. I shall give one example from

Psalm 15:2–3, which is part of the answer to the opening question of the psalm, about who is permitted to enter the sanctuary. Two ways of understanding the logic of the text may be seen in the fact that the text can be arranged in different ways in terms of the balance of the cola. One possibility for arranging the text, and the one followed, for example, in *The Psalms*, a new translation prepared for use in worship in the Church of England (London, 1977), is,

A   Whoever walks blamelessly   (2a)
B   and does what is right,   (2b)
A   Whoever speaks truth in one's heart,   (2c)
B   and has not slandered with one's tongue,   (3a)
A   Whoever has not done evil to one's friend   (3b)
B   nor lifted up a taunt against one's neighbor.   (3c)
                                                     (my trans.)

The text here is arranged as a series of bicola, that is, two-part lines. The first one (2a and b) recognizes that the two participial constructions of which it is composed in Hebrew are precisely balanced (meter, length, and syntax). Verses 2c and 3a balance each other as positive and negative expressions in length, meter, and meaning—the last in the fact that both cola have to do with the realm of speech and both deal with that by referring to a part of the body as the source or instrument of the speaking ("one's heart"/"one's tongue"). The final two cola (3b and c) are clearly balanced in terms of length and meter as well as meaning. The key terms that bind the cola together and indicate their particular focus are the terms "friend" and "neighbor."

Such an understanding of the arrangement of these verses not only yields an intricate and careful symmetry, but it also leads to a way of understanding the progress of thought. The first bicolon (2a and b) is composed of parallel cola giving *general statements of right conduct*. The verbs "walk" and "do" characterize general or overall behavior and "blamelessly" and "right" are in like manner general or broad terms for right or righteous living. The second bicolon (2c and 3a) begins the *particular or concrete explication* of the general conduct described in 2a and b. The first specification of righteousness and blamelessness, therefore, has to do with *the morality of speech*, what one does and does not say. The positively formulated description of proper speaking in the A colon calls for speaking truthfully from or in one's heart. The negative parallel colon (B) takes the specification further by describing the right worshiper as one who has not used the tongue to slander. The second characteristic of right conduct (3b and c) has to do with *proper relationship with one's neighbor*, which means neither *doing* anything bad to another person (A colon) nor *saying* anything bad against a neighbor (B colon).

But there are aspects of the poetic form and character of these verses that stand in tension with this arrangement or fail to be highlighted as a result of it. Another way of viewing the text that is very close to the RSV arrangement is as follows.

A   Whoever walks blamelessly,   (2a)
B   does what is right,   (2b)
C   and speaks truth in one's heart;   (2c)
A   Whoever has not slandered with one's tongue,   (3a)
B   has not done evil to one's friend,   (3b)
C   nor lifted up a taunt against one's neighbor.   (3a)

Now the text is seen to be composed of two tricola rather than three bicola. The tricola are each balanced by being composed of three cola containing closely parallel syntactic structures: in v. 2 a series of masculine singular participles in the Hebrew ("walking," "doing," "speaking") with abstract nouns of moral quality as objects ("blamelessness," "right," "truth"); and in v. 3 a series of finite negative verbs ("has not slandered," "has not done evil," "nor taunted") plus prepositional phrases ("with one's tongue," "to one's friend," "against one's neighbor").

All the participles of v. 2 describe right conduct in a *general* or *abstract* fashion: walking blamelessly, doing righteousness, speaking truth. The negative clauses of v. 3 then go on to describe *more specific* or *concrete* actions that begin to spell out the content or details of v. 2. The first concerns what one has done in speech; the second with how one behaves toward another person; the third with one's attitude and manner of speech vis à vis someone else. Each of the negative clauses in v. 3 balances each of the participial clauses in v. 2 and in the same order. That is immediately clear with the second and third examples in each case: the negative specification of *doing* right is *not doing* evil against a neighbor, and the negative specification of *speaking* truth is *not speaking* taunting, arrogant words against someone else. But this correlation of participle and negative verb also reaches back to the initial example (2a and 3a). The verb for "slander" (*ragal*) is derived from the noun for "foot" (*regel*) and thus means something like "foot it" or "go about." The verb thus neatly balances the first participle: The negative specification of *walking/going* blamelessly is *not going with one's tongue*.

It is hoped that the above discussion of Ps. 15:2–3 shows how fairly simple but careful attention to poetic features, in this case especially *am-*

biguity and *balance*, opens up the richness of the text that is both aesthetic and instructive. The final poetic feature that I want to highlight for the work of the interpreter is *metaphor* (cf. the discussion in chap. 2), where one thing is characterized by describing it as something else, the something else thus giving us a clue to how we should view or understand the thing itself, as for example, when a lamenter describes himself or herself as surrounded by wild animals (cf. chap. 2 and the exposition of Psalm 22 in Part 2). What is being talked about is people, but picturing them or speaking of them as though they were wild animals closing in on prey depicts the plight of the lamenter more vividly than an abstract discussion of that plight might. Similar to metaphor is the *simile*, where one thing is said to be *like* something else. Similarity rather than identity is the point made by a simile.[6] In Ps. 64:2–4, simile and metaphor join together to create an ominous imagery. The psalm speaks of the scheming of evildoers,

> who whet their tongues *like swords* [simile]
> who aim bitter words *like arrows* [simile]
> (v. 3)

> shooting from ambush at the blameless [metaphor],
> shooting suddenly and without fear [metaphor].
> (v. 4)

Rather than simply saying that wicked people are scheming against the psalmist, the poet compares their tongues to sharp swords—we speak of a cutting tongue—and their words to arrows. Sensitive interpreters can immediately recall occasions when words cut into them almost physically or they felt struck by ugly words with the force of a stone against the body. The simile communicates the impact of the schemes with power, as does the metaphor of the ambush where someone unsuspecting is done in by those who hide, attack suddenly and unexpectedly, and escape.

The psalms are filled with such images, and (see chap. 2) they provide a frequent point of contact with human experience or offer a concreteness, an illustration of a point, that when brought out and exploited in the act of interpretation can aid in both hearing and feeling the psalms,

---

6. Laurence Perrine in his book *Sound and Sense* (New York: Harcourt, Brace & Co., 1956), 49, helpfully distinguishes simile from metaphor as follows: "In the simile the comparison is expressed by use of some word such as *like, as, then, similar to* or *resembles.* In a metaphor the comparison is implied; that is, the figurative term is *substituted for* or *identified with* the literal term."

in the didactic and the aesthetic appropriation. In chapter 2 the focus was heavily on those ways of speaking that touch base with the human situation, the human need. But metaphor and simile occur in many contexts. Indeed they play a primary role in the way the psalms convey aspects of the individual's relationship with God. A number of examples come quickly to mind: the tree by the water versus the chaff in Psalm 1 (see the exposition of Psalm 1 in Part 2), the green olive tree in the house of God (Ps. 52:8), the shepherd and the flock (e.g., Pss. 23,. 74:1), God as a high rock and strong tower giving security against the enemy (e.g., Ps. 61:2–3), and God as a bird whose wings provide shadow and protection (Pss. 17:8; 36:7; 57:1; 61:4; 63:7; 91:4).

The poetry of the psalms is far too rich to explicate in a single chapter, or even a single book. But careful attention to poetic features such as the ones discussed and illustrated here has the effect of opening up dimensions of both beauty and meaning as well as giving the interpreter language and images that help make clear, vivid, and concrete the message of the individual psalms. To the extent that one listens to, examines, even caresses such imagery to get its feel and help others do the same, to that extent the psalms will catch the heart and mind of those who read and hear.[7]

---

7. For a helpful extended discussion of the imagery of Scripture see G. B. Caird, *The Language and Imagery of the Bible* (Philadelphia: Westminster Press, 1980).

4. TROUBLE AND WOE: INTERPRETING THE BIBLICAL LAMENTS

Some important dimensions of the theology of the laments or ways in which they may resonate with human experience are discussed in chapter 1 with reference to the works of Rainier Albertz, Walter Brueggemann, Erhard Gerstenberger, Claus Westermann, and others. In this chapter I want to elaborate an approach suggested briefly earlier (p. 8) as *one* way of working with the laments. The reader ought to read more widely in the literature mentioned in chapter 1 to enrich his or her appropriation and communication of the biblical laments.

The reader of the psalms of the Old Testament is quickly struck by the fact that most of the psalms deal with some sort of trouble or adversity, the psalmists' experiences of enmity, oppression, and wickedness. As I have indicated earlier, it is not always clear what the trouble of the psalmist is or was, or who the enemy and the wicked are. Indeed the particularities of the situation of the one who prays are often difficult to discern. What is going on? Who are the enemies? Why are they hostile to the one praying? What have they done that is bad? What is personally happening to the psalmist that is regularly described in extreme terms?

Westermann has recently and properly reiterated the point that in the structure of the psalm of lament, one is usually dealing with three dimensions. "It is directed toward God (an accusation or complaint against God), toward other men (a complaint against an enemy), and toward the lamenter himself (I-lament or We-lament)."[1] Recognition of

1. Claus Westermann, "The Role of the Lament in the Theology of the Old Testament," *Interpretation* 28 (1974): 27 [= *Praise and Lament in the Psalms* (Atlanta: John Knox Press, 1981), 267].

these components, however, does not answer the questions raised about the psalmist's situation; it even raises other questions. Sometimes one of these components is not present. Even more important is the fact that the relationship of the three dimensions to one another is often not very clear and interpretation founders on the effort to understand that relationship.

Take Psalm 6 as an example. The psalm begins with a plea directed to God that immediately identifies God as the psalmist's problem—the anger and rebuke of God. The one praying seeks to avoid having to live under the divine wrath. In various ways the plight of the psalmist is further described as an internal matter: languishing, with bones troubled, near death, needing healing, moaning, and weeping. Then suddenly this apparently physical condition, which sounds like sickness of some sort, is related to external forces. The eye wastes away because of vexation, grows weak because of "all my foes." The psalm ends in the plea and confidence that God will put the enemy to flight and to shame.

Typically in the modern study of the psalms, and to some extent in the precritical period, interpreters have tried to pin down a psalm such as this one, or groups of psalms, to one particular reference, use, or moment. Historical criticism has tried to determine, for a particular psalm and the situation it describes, who spoke these words and what had happened to them. In so doing one seeks to determine the occasion of the psalm's composition as a chief clue to understanding its various parts and the relation of the parts to one another. The form-critical and cult-functional approaches have sought to uncover as the chief clue to interpretation the setting and the moment in the activity of the cult when a particular psalm appropriately fit. Thus efforts have been made to determine if the subject of a psalm is David or some other historical figure, or one has claimed that the subject is a king, a person falsely accused in court, the exilic community, and so on.

This effort to locate in some fashion the persons and the problems of the laments has been especially characteristic of discussions about the evildoers or the enemies in the psalms. A number of extended treatments of the question of the identity of these persons or groups have been put forth in this century.[2] The earlier works tended to identify a

2. Among the primary works dealing with this subject are the following: Sigmund Mowinckel, *Psalmenstudien I* (Oslo, 1921–24); idem, *The Psalms in Israel's Worship* (Nashville: Abingdon Press, 1962); Hans Schmidt, *Das Gebet des Angeklagten im Alten Testament* (Giessen, 1928); Harris Birkeland, *Die Feinde des Individuums in der Israelitischen Psalmenliteratur* (Oslo, 1933); idem, *The Evildoers in the Book of Psalms* (Oslo, 1955); Othmar Keel, *Feinde und*

particular category or group as the enemy or the doer of evil in the psalms; for example, Hans Schmidt contended that the enemies in a number of psalms are false accusers of the one lamenting, pleading to God for justice; Sigmund Mowinckel held the early view that the enemies were sorcerers and demonic forces; and H. Birkeland claimed that most of the individual laments are songs of the king and that the enemies are national enemies opposing the rule of the king.

While efforts to identify a particular type or group as the enemies of the individual or the nation in the psalms, and efforts to identify the institutional setting of the individual laments and thus determine the identity of the enemies, continue to come forth—for example, in Walter Beyerlin's modification of Schmidt's thesis—it seems less and less likely that interpreters will uncover a particular identity for these opponents and evildoers. The very nature of the psalms and the language with which such persons are described both obscure the immediate identification of the enemies and at the same time suggest that they may have many identities. The individual laments are in many ways strongly stereotypical. That is, in moving from one lament to the other, one can encounter much of the same structure and content repeated, with some variation in the images and primary metaphors used. The enemies themselves are talked about in very typical stereotyped language. Clichés of all sorts are used throughout the psalms. The opponents are described in stark terms, usually with strong language and negative imagery. This stereotypical language should suggest caution in assuming that there is a single referent for the enemies or evildoers. Animal metaphors, war terminology, the language of the hunt can all be used to express the same reality. The adversaries seem to be characterized in the same way no matter what their actuality is for the one who sings or prays.

This situation, however, which confounds the best efforts of interpreters of the psalms, has its positive consequence. It leaves an openness for understanding who these enemies are in a way that pinning them down to one particular category, group, or type of person within the community would not. That is, the enemies are in fact whoever the enemies are for the singers of the psalms. Should one determine that

Gottesleugner: Studien zum Image der Widersacher in den Individualpsalmen (Stuttgart, 1969); Walter Beyerlin, *Die Rettung der Bedrängten in den Feindepsalmen der Einzelnen auf Institutionelle Zusammenhänge Untersucht* (Göttingen: Vandenhoeck & Ruprecht, 1970); Lothar Ruppert, *Die Leidende Gerechte und Seine Feinde* (Würzburg: Echter Verlag, 1973); H. J. Kraus, *Theologie der Psalmen* (Neukirchen-Vluyn: Neukirchener Verlag, 1979).

most of the evildoers are sorcerers or false accusers, then the laments to some degree become capable of being appropriated only by those who are in a comparable situation, that is, who are faced with sorcerers or false accusers. But that is not necessarily the case. The laments become appropriate for persons who cry out to God in all kinds of situations in which they may encounter various kinds of opposition. The strong, stark language with which the opponents are described also should not be misleading at this point. Once again, the interpreter needs to be aware of the poetic character of the laments and the dominance of cliché and stereotypical language. The degree of opposition or moral culpability of the opponent is not determined by the intensity of the lament or the passion and strength of language. The psalmists clearly appropriate typical descriptive terminology to speak about those whom they perceive as persons giving them trouble in one way or another or standing against God.

The point I am stressing with regard to the laments is the one made more generally in chapter 2 with regard to all the psalms—that is, that the language of the psalms is *open* and *metaphorical*. That recognition is one of the most important hermeneutical clues to the interpretation of the psalms, as well as an indication of why the psalms for generations have served so effectively as the hymnody for various religious communities. In many respects the effort to identify in some sharp and specific way who the individuals are who speak or are spoken about in the psalm, whether they are the "I," the "we," the enemies, or whoever, is a move in precisely the opposite direction from those interpretive efforts that will make the psalms more responsive to contemporary appropriation. While the extensive work in this century on the cultic interpretation of the psalms has been an exciting enterprise that has often uncovered something of their original cultic context, that effort has been of very little use for the contemporary interpreter who asks the meaning of the psalms in the present community of faith. The open language of the psalms invites, allows, and calls for interpretation that looks and moves forward into the present and the future as well as for interpretation that looks backward. The former is well indicated by the extensive use of the psalms in the effort of the early Christian community to understand the reality and meaning of Jesus of Nazareth. The connections are fairly easy to see as one reads the New Testament, and they are not difficult for the later interpreter to understand and even accept (see chap. 2). The problems inherent in the relationship of prophecy and fulfillment are less noticeable when the psalms are taken up. That is precisely because their language is open and capable of coming to actualization in many contexts without seeming to violate the intention of the composition at an earlier stage. In similar fashion, the homiletical and nonliteral rabbinic expositions of the psalms in Midrash Tehillim not infrequently have a certain validity and sensibility to them because of the freedom that is inherent in the language.

That openness to varieties of application and actualization continues through the history of interpretation into the present. One has only to peruse the collection of historical bits and pieces in R. E. Prothero's *The Psalms in Human Life* to see how easily this happens, and how frequently the contemporary reader of the psalms not only can understand how they were related to the situation in the past but indeed is willing to agree to that understanding because of the universality and commonality of their metaphorical language. That situation is no different in the present from what it was in the past, a fact that opens up the hermeneutical possibilities for the psalms to be related to the life and experience of the contemporary congregation or the contemporary believer. That is true as much for the trouble of the lamenter and the phenomenon of the enemies as it is for other dimensions and components of the psalms (see chap. 2). The enemies are an open category, and the content of the category is filled by the predicament and plight not only of the psalmist but also of the contemporary singer of the psalm.

This does not mean, however, that one cannot move backward to gain some clues about the earlier actualization of the psalms or earlier points of reference that will help in the contemporary appropriation of them, that is, in understanding what they are talking about or are capable of talking and praying about. Indeed, that is the other primary interpretive suggestion I want to make, although it moves in a somewhat different direction than indicated by the remarks above about the open and metaphorical character of the laments. While that openness and the rich stereotypical and figurative language enable the psalms to move forward into many different possibilities for a contemporary resonance with the situations and petitions of the lament, that character also creates possibilities for relationships between the laments and the past experiences of the community of faith that may be both illuminating and heuristic. Such looking backward into the text, however, may be more usefully and helpfully done by *relating the laments to narrative and historical context* than by simply examining in as exhaustive a fashion as possible the language of the laments themselves. The latter has been a tendency in most of the studies of the enemies or evildoers in the psalms, with scholars examining in detail the various expressions or terms for the enemies and the evildoers and the particular contexts in which they occur in the psalms, in order to try to understand to what or to whom they refer. More fruitful results may come from moving outside the Psalter to seek some concrete picture or possible references for the individuals or groups alluded to in the psalms, that is, to find those occasions or moments in which such words were or would have been appropriate. In the narrative and prophetic books one may find clues to the interpretation, or perhaps better put, illustrations of the applicability of the forms and language, of the psalms, which may be of continuing relevance in contemporary interpretation.

It is clear that a step in that direction has already been made by the historical superscriptions to the psalms (see chap. 2). Those superscriptions that refer to specific moments and events in the life of David are a way of saying that the psalm over which the superscription is written makes sense in just such a context. An obvious example of this is Psalm 51 with its allusion to the Bathsheba incident. The superscription does not force one to confine the power of those words to that occasion alone, but it does illustrate with power where such words of passionate self-condemnation and extreme plea for transformation and cleansing are appropriate. The setting of that psalm against the context of the taking of Bathsheba by David is certainly not without justification in the light of what one actually encounters in the psalms. This is not to make the claim that the psalm was composed by David on the occasion. A decision or judgment about that is largely irrelevant. Whether composed then or not, there is much in the psalm that seems to make sense in relationship to that incident. One of the correspondences is obviously the fact that the depth of the sin confessed in Psalm 51 seems to match the depth of the sin committed by David. Clearly one of the primary reasons for the association of David with the psalm is the relationship between the psalmist's declaration "against you, you only have I sinned" (v. 4) and David's very straightforward response to Nathan's extended announcement of the Lord's judgment when David says simply, "I have sinned against the Lord [ḥāṭā' tî lyhwh]" (2 Sam. 12:13). One may assume that in Psalm 51 the sins committed by the psalmist have had effect upon other persons, but they are seen entirely as sin against God. In the same manner does David speak about his acts.

That correspondence between David's actions and the actions of the psalmist is, of course, demonstrated further in the relationship of the parallel colon in 51:4 to the divine word of judgment. The psalmist declares, "I have done evil in your eyes." Nathan/the Lord says to David, "Why have you despised the word of the Lord to do evil in his/my eyes?" So both the accusation and the response are couched in the same language in Psalm 51 and 2 Samuel 12. One notes further that the primary vehicle for the theme of Psalm 51 is the root *ht'*. The vocabulary for sin is used extensively in this psalm: it occurs in seven different verses (4, 5, 6, 7, 9, 11, 15).[3] In all seven of those verses, some nominal or verbal form of the root *ht'* is used, matched by several other typical words for sin. This thematic use of the root *ht'* corresponds to the use of that same root in David's confession: "I have sinned [*ḥāṭā'tî*] against the Lord."

Finally, when the question of the three dimensions—God, lamenter, enemies—is raised, one notes immediately the total absence of the enemies in Psalm 51, which corresponds fully and appropriately to the situation set as a background or illustration of the psalm. The occasion of these words, if it is the David and Bathsheba incident, is an occasion that has to do with the Lord and David and not with any adversaries. The enemies are absent from the psalm as indeed they were absent from the situation described in the superscription. The same thing is true in another case, that of Hezekiah's psalm in Isaiah 38. The lament expressions there are set against the context of a sickness of Hezekiah rather than the problem of enemies, and indeed the enemies do not occur within the psalm itself.

One of the most common complaints in the psalms is against those who taunt (*ḥārap*) the lamenter, God, or the people. When one looks at such narrative contexts as Judges 8:15; Neh. 4:2–4; 6:13; 1 Samuel 17; 1 Samuel 25; and 2 Kings 19, as well as the context in which taunting is referred to in the psalms, it is clear that one or many are challenging or questioning the power of the Lord because of the powerlessness of God's servants or people. The men of Succoth and Penuel taunt Gideon: "Are Zebah and Zalmuna already in your hand that we should give you bread?" He has not yet captured the kings of Midian, they clearly do not think he will, so the men see no need to do what he asks. Nehemiah and the Judeans are taunted by Sanballat and Tobiah, whose rhetorical questions clearly scoff at the capabilities of the people to restore the walls and the city. Appropriately, Nehemiah responds with a lament and a plea to God to send his enemies into captivity. In a similar way, David's request

3. Cf. Patrick D. Miller, Jr., "Studies in Hebrew Word Patterns," *Harvard Theological Review* 73 (1981): 79–89.

to Nabal for food for his men is met with the scoffing question "Who is David? Who is the son of Jesse?" (1 Sam. 25:10). In the story of David's battle with Goliath, the Philistine warrior taunts the Israelites and then David for their powerlessness against his might. Again the taunt comes in a question, "Am I a dog, that you come to me with sticks?" David correctly perceives Goliath's taunts as a challenge to the power of God, which is overcome only when he demonstrates the Lord's greater power by killing Goliath. Finally, the speech of the Rabshakeh representing the Assyrian king to the besieged Hezekiah is described by both Hezekiah and the Lord as taunting the living God. The context of that taunt is, of course, a challenge to the Lord's power to deliver the people from Sennacherib: "Has any of the gods of the nations ever delivered his land out of the hands of the king of Assyria? Where are the gods of Hamath and Arpad? . . . Who among all the gods of the countries have delivered their countries out of my hand that the Lord should deliver Jerusalem out of my hand?" (2 Kings 18:33–35). When one compares these incidents with such Psalms as 42, 69, 74, and 79, one sees that the taunts received by the lamenters of the psalms are essentially a challenge or mockery of their helplessness and the powerlessness of their God to do anything about their situation. The taunt is embodied particularly in rhetorical questions, and especially the question, Where is your God? (Pss. 42:10; 79:10) or its equivalent. The adversaries who taunt may be in outright conflict with the Lord's people or their representative, as in the case of Goliath, the Rabshakeh, and Sanballat and Tobiah; or they may manifest their opposition as a third party refusing to aid and support, as in the case of Nabal and the men of Succoth and Penuel. These stories thus offer us clues for understanding the laments by suggesting the kinds of opposition to which the laments allude and giving us some indication of the sorts of contexts that would have been in mind or appropriate for those psalms that cry out against the taunters of the Lord and the people.[4] One may be no closer to the actual situation that originally brought forth any one of these laments, but the interpreter is given a wealth of illustrative possibilities for uncovering contexts for these stereotypical expressions. Further, the openness of the laments themselves leads the reader to seek their resonance with contemporary experience not just in general experiences of insults and taunts, as one thinks of children on a playground, but in those occasions where personal and

---

4. For a similar use of *ḥārap* in inscriptions from Iron Age Palestine see Patrick D. Miller, "Psalms and Inscriptions," in *Congress Volume, Vienna 1980*, ed. J. A. Emerton (Leiden, E. J. Brill, 1981), 311–32.

corporate existence raise questions out of one's sense of helplessness and about the power of God in human life where forces within and without are overwhelming.

One of the texts that is most illuminating and instructive for thinking about the laments, and particularly the enemy or the evildoer, is the story of Hannah in 1 Samuel 1. That narrative manifests significant interaction with the psalms of lament. For illustration, one can compare 1 Samuel 1 with Psalm 6, although this psalm would certainly not be the only place where one finds significant correlation. Hannah's problem, the source of her complaint or lament, is clearly indicated in the story. She is barren. She speaks of that barrenness as affliction (*'ŏnî*), typical terminology for describing the plight of lamenters (Pss. 9:12; 25:18; 31:7; 44:24; 88:9; Lam. 1:3, 7; 3:1, 19). But when one looks more closely at the details of the story, it is clear that the complaint and the situation are not simply one-dimensional, having to do only with the internal plight of the lamenter, that is, her barrenness, but are indeed three-dimensional in exactly the way Westermann has suggested. And all three dimensions or components of the lament are held together in a singular reality. As in Psalm 6 and most of the other laments, the crisis of the complaint has its roots in part in the action of God, in part in the internal situation of the lamenter, and in part in the activity of other persons. The agency of God in bringing about the cause of the complaint is specifically indicated in v. 5 with the clause, "because Yahweh had closed her womb." This is not elaborated at any length, but the complaint is directed to God in part because, as is the case with the laments generally, God is in part the problem and the creator of her suffering situation, as indeed the singer of Psalm 6 finds God the source of his or her internal suffering as well as the source of its resolution.[5]

Hannah is also confronted with a very real enemy, Peninnah, the other wife of Elkanah. The word *ṣārāh* in v. 6 may be understood as a technical term for "rival wife," as most modern commentators have interpreted it, but it is hardly coincidental that this is the feminine form of one of the most common terms for adversary in the laments (e.g., in Pss. 3:1; 13:4; 27:2). Even more important, Peninnah's hostile action against Hannah is specifically cited. Verse 6 indicates that Peninnah vexed

5. As this discussion and chap. 2 indicate, I find the effort to determine whether or not Psalm 6 reflects actual physical illness a fruitless endeavor. All the language used in this psalm is as fully capable of being used figuratively as literally, including and perhaps especially the verb *rāpā'*. One should not exclude sickness as an appropriate context for singing this lament. Precisely the juxtaposition of the lament against a text like 1 Samuel 1 opens up other ways of understanding this kind of language (chap. 2).

(*ka'as*) Hannah, and in v. 16 Hannah alludes to her vexation as the reason for her prayer. The same terminology is used in Ps. 6:7 to describe the plight of the psalmist there, that is, vexation (*ka'as*), which has been created because of the psalmist's foes (*ṣôrʿray*; cf. the similar expressions and the collocation of *ka'as* and *ṣar* in Ps. 31:9). One may assume that the vexation of Hannah's enemy is not unlike the taunting (*ḥerpāh*) discussed above, where the enemy is described as one who mocks the psalmist because God is not present, or not willing, or unable to deliver the lamenter from his or her plight. In every sense, Peninnah is the "maker of trouble," to use the language of Psalm 6 (*pōʿālê 'āwen*; v. 8). Peninnah may not bear the customary visage of the enemies of the psalms as we usually think of them, using the categories of opposing parties, sorcerers, unjust oppressors in the court, and the like, but that is just the point. The enemy of the lamenter is the one who is indeed the adversary of the one who complains. And whatever the language or however strong the tone, the category of the enemies is broad and can include a rival wife.

When, therefore, we have difficulty integrating the three dimensions into a single notion, that is, understanding how the psalms of lament at one and the same time can talk about the problem's being internal (self), external (enemy), and divine (God), a story such as that of Hannah helps us see how these facets hold together and make sense.

Although this takes us outside the Book of Psalms, the other primary collection of laments in the Old Testament, the so-called confessions of Jeremiah (11:18—12:6; 15:10–12, 15–21; 17:14–18; 18:18–23; 20:7–13, 14–18), provides a further example of the way in which narrative setting or context illumines the possible understanding or the referential possibilities of the enemies in the laments and the situation of the one who complains vis-à-vis God, self, and the adversaries. The resonance between Jeremiah's complaints and the psalms has been well recognized.[6] Indeed there has been vigorous discussion on two issues arising out of the obvious relationship of the language of the laments of Jeremiah and of those of the psalms:

1. The question of the dependence of one set of laments or complaints on the other; that is, were Jeremiah's laments modeled on the form and

---

6. The basic study in the modern period is W. Baumgartner's *Die Klagegedichte des Jeremia* (Giessen: A. Töpelmann, 1917). See also P. E. Bonnard, *Le Psautier selon Jeremie* (Paris: Editions du Cerf, 1960); H. Graf Reventlow, *Liturgie und prophetisches Ich bei Jeremia* (Gutersloh: Gerd Mohn, 1963); and most recently, R. P. Carroll, *From Chaos to Covenant: Prophecy in the Book of Jeremiah* (New York: Crossroad, 1981), 107–35.

language of psalms of lament (as, e.g., W. Baumgartner suggests) or did the former influence the latter (as, e.g., P. E. Bonnard thinks)?

2. The question of the relationship of Jeremiah's confession to the liturgy of the cult and to his own life; that is, are they liturgical pieces arising out of and uttered in the context of the cult (the position of H. Graf Reventlow), or do they reflect the experience of the prophet who uses conventional forms and language to articulate his anguish (that of John Bright)?[7] Robert Carroll has taken something of a middle position on the latter issue, seeing a heavy redactional influence on the confessions to create two approaches to the life of the prophet, one that sees the prophet as an intercessor for the nation and one that sees the prophet as persecuted and opposed by the community (see n. 6). At one point he suggests that the "linking of the formal lament style with the men of Anathoth (Jer. 11:21–23)" may suggest "a redactional attempt to relate such motifs to the life of Jeremiah (on the analogy of the psalm titles, which relate formal cultic elements to the life of David the king)."[8] This possibility would indeed seem to describe what has happened with Jeremiah's laments, and the analogy with the psalm titles is appropriate. Whether the relation of the language of the laments to Jeremiah's life is an original, that is, biographical datum, or a redactional move is, however, irrelevant to the point being raised here. A context in narrative is provided that serves to illumine and illustrate where and how lament language is appropriate.

Jeremiah's complaint is against God, and God is his problem. He brings an accusation against the Lord (12:1). But the Lord's role is very clear from the narrative and indeed from allusions in some of the laments. God has laid on Jeremiah the burden of the prophetic call, so that he cannot let it go on no matter what the opposition. The Lord is indeed the cause of his distress, as is frequently the case in the laments. In this instance, however, we do not have a lamenter who feels God's judgment because of sin or assumes that God has closed the womb and made barren, as in the case of Hannah. The problem is quite a different matter here. It is in response to the call of and in the service of the Lord that the lamenter now feels put upon.

Jeremiah's personal plight is described in a variety of ways typical of

7. John Bright, "Jeremiah's Complaints: Liturgy or Expressions of Personal Distress?" in *Proclamation and Presence*, ed. J. I. Durham and J. R. Porter (Richmond: John Knox Press, 1970), 189–214.

8. Carroll, *From Chaos to Covenant*, 109.

laments.[9] He sits alone (*bādad yāšabtî*) because of the hand of the Lord. The particular idiom here is not a common one. It does occur once in lament context referring to the loneliness of destroyed Jerusalem (Lam. 1:1). The portrayal, however, of isolation from the community is given in other ways in the laments; usually it is a result, apparently, of sickness (see Lev. 13:45; Pss. 31:11; 88:8, 18; Job 19:13–22; 30:9–23). In like manner the hand of the Lord bringing distress that may be sickness is also found in the laments (Pss. 32:4; 38:2; 39:10).[10] But in Jeremiah's case a notion that appears in the laments and that apart from its context would probably imply what isolation and the hand of.the Lord customarily suggest, that is, sickness, carries a different force and meaning because of the story context that the Book of Jeremiah gives to it. It is clear that he sits alone in isolation from the community because of his prophetic task. His message receives widespread opposition and resistance, even from his closest friends and family (11:21–23; 20:10).

The use of a motif (if not the actual language) associated with illness is not surprising in light of the fact that one of the laments refers to unceasing pain and an incurable wound (15:18) and in another instance Jeremiah prays to God for healing. Language and references to illness are so common in the lament of the Old Testament that there is no need to cite examples. The case of Jeremiah's laments, however, again makes clear how determinative the situation of the lamenter is for understanding the reference of the sickness-healing language. It is clearly in this case a metaphorical way to describe Jeremiah's anguish and distress, his "affliction" if one may call it that, a distress that, like wickedness, is caused in part by God. One is reminded again, therefore, of the openness of the language and imagery. Sickness is a universal and vivid image to describe situations of extreme distress. The actual circumstances of sickness may not be present at all, but deliverance from distress is a healing. Jeremiah's "sickness" is his personal anguish at being under attack from all sides, either verbally (18:18) or actually, and thus being separated and rejected by much of the community, including those close to him.

When one asks about the enemies in the laments of Jeremiah, one encounters much stereotypical language to describe them, language that is

9. There is no attempt here to give all the possible connections to the style and language of the psalms of lament. The details of these associations are provided in the works of Baumgartner, Reventlow, and Carroll. The examples mentioned here illustrate the way typical lament language gets its content and particularity out of the context.

10. John Bright, in "Jeremiah's Complaints," argues that the expression *bādad yāšabtî* precludes any association with the idea of isolation because of sickness.

characteristic of laments in general. They are often identified with general, anonymous language: "they," "them," "many," "my persecutors," and the like. "They speak" taunting words to Jeremiah as in the laments (e.g., Pss. 3:2; 40:15; 70:3).

All of this stereotypical language, however, is now placed in a context that serves to give content and reference to the clichés. That context is at two levels, both of which serve to flesh out the meaning of the lamenter's anguished cries and prayers. One level is provided by the immediate context of the laments, where information is given just before or after, that clearly is intended to relate to them. This information may be, indeed probably is, on the redactional level, as Carroll and others suggest. But it intends to give the reader some context for interpreting these particular laments that in form and style are like so many others. This contextual level is provided specifically by 11:21–23; 12:5–6; 18:18; and 20:1–6. All these passages flow directly into or out of the laments and guide the reader. The other level is the book itself; that is, these laments are set directly in the Book of Jeremiah, which contains a store of biographical data. Again the reader hears the laments, as I have already indicated above, not as some general words but as Jeremiah's cries to be heard and interpreted in the light of his experience.

In the first laments in chapters 11 and 12, Jeremiah cries out against the wicked and those who would take his life. The imagery of the lamb led to the slaughter is familiar from Ps. 44:11 and 22; and the quoted threat to kill him so that his name be remembered no more, is both generally present in the laments in the constant sense of threat to life from the enemy and specifically there in Ps. 83:4 as plotters conspire together to do in the lamenters so that the name is remembered no more. But what is clear from the context (i.e., from 11:21–23 and 12:6) is that these persons who threaten Jeremiah's life are not anonymous or unknown; nor is the language in this case metaphorical. Jeremiah's life really is threatened, and the enemy is his family (cf. Ps. 69:8). Alienation from family is not merely a way of expressing total isolation—though such expressions may function that way in a lament when it is heard or viewed in another context—but a reality certainly tied to the way in which Jeremiah's words were perceived as threatening to the priestly establishment of which Jeremiah's family was a part. The fear of those who "seek to take one's life" is a common element in the laments (Pss. 35:4; 38:12; 40:14; 54:3; 63:9; 70:2; 86:14; cf. 31:13). In the instance of Jeremiah, as we may assume was frequently the case when the laments of the psalms were used, his life was genuinely in danger; and there were those within his family and elsewhere who "dealt treacherously" (12:1, 6) with him (cf. Lam. 1:2; Pss. 25:3; 59:5; Hab. 1:3) and "sought to take his life" (11:21; 38:16).

In Jeremiah 11:19 the prophet laments that "they devised schemes against me," an accusation familiar in the laments of the psalms (10:2; 35:4; 41:7; 140:2). The context of the second lament (Jer. 18:18) makes clear that there really were plots against Jeremiah, presumably on the part of the leaders of the community and specifically the priests, the wise or scribes, and the prophets who are referred to in 18:18. The rest of the Book of Jeremiah also indicates that he often proclaimed a word against priests, wise men, and prophets (e.g., 8:8–12; 9:23–24; 20:1–6; 23; 27—29) and that they and other leaders plotted against him (20:2; 26:7–8; 36:26; 38:4–6). Thus Jeremiah experiences imprisonment, beatings, and efforts to have him killed. It is about these sufferings that he complains to God. A further connection to the wise men is seen in the prayer of Jeremiah that "they" might be ashamed and dismayed (17: 17–18) and in the oracle against them in 8:8–13, which announces that just such a fate will be theirs.

Jeremiah claims also to have been taunted by his enemies (15:15; 20:8), and indeed that is the case. Similar to the familiar *ḥerpāh* of the psalms and elsewhere comes the taunt to Jeremiah that is peculiarly appropriate to his situation: "Where is the word of the Lord? Let it come" (17:15). Jeremiah himself at one point says quite clearly that the true prophet is the one whose word comes to pass (28:9) and indeed that was the claim of Deuteronomy (18:22).[11] So the characteristic taunt of the enemy is in Jeremiah's case specifically tied to the issue of true and false prophecy, and the prophets of peace (*šālôm*), an issue that represented a major conflict in his career.

Another example of the context's giving a particular force to typical words in the lament is in the reference to "terror on every side" (*māgôr missābîb*) in 20:10. *Māgôr missābîb* is a characteristic formula in Jeremiah (6:25; 20:3; 46:5; 49:29), occurring elsewhere only in Ps. 31:13 and Lam. 2:22. When the "many" pick this up in the context of 20:10, it reflects their report against him, that this is characteristic of his prophecy. They hope that he will be deceived and proved wrong so that they can do him in. In this case, therefore, *māgôr missābîb* reflects Jeremiah's situation, as one would expect in a lament, but it also is the word of Jeremiah being thrown back at him. In the light of 20:6, the immediate context, it may

11. See Bright, "Jeremiah's Complaints," 205–7.

also be—as others have suggested—a derogatory nickname that has been given to Jeremiah. Even as he has renamed Pashur "Terror on Every Side," so now he is being given the same destructive title by others.

The final example of typical lament language about the actions of the lamenters that is given a particular meaning or force in the context of Jeremiah is the image of the pit that is dug by the enemy to take, or do in, the one who laments to God. Twice Jeremiah uses this image (18:20, 22). The expression for "pit" here is *šîḥāh/šûḥāh*. That word is used in this imagery in the laments (Ps. 57:6). The same imagery appears with the word *bôr* in Ps. 7:15. Alongside this metaphor is the figure of the pit (*bôr*) that is the final destiny or fate of the lamenter if God does not come to rescue (Pss. 28:1; 30:3; 69:15; 88:4, 6; 143:7; Isa. 38:18). In a song of thanksgiving the psalmist gives praise to God for having lifted him up from the pit (*bôr*), from the mire (*ṭîṭ yāwēn*), presumably the divine response to the type of cry one finds in Ps. 69:14–15. In the Book of Jeremiah the use of this stereotypical language as it is reflected in 18:20 and 22 has a vivid and precise force. The metaphor becomes literalized in the experience of Jeremiah. The interpreter of the psalms is not likely to interpret this image literally in the various places where it occurs, but Jeremiah presses us to do just that in that context. For one of the most threatening occasions in his life, according to the story we are told, is when Zedekiah had him put in a dungeon (*bêt habbôr*; 37:16) and then removed from there and lowered into a cistern where he sank (*wayitbaʿ*) in the mire (*ṭîṭ*) (38:6). The picture of Jeremiah is precisely that of the laments, only it is no mere image in this instance. Jeremiah is cast into a pit by his enemies (Pss. 57:6; 69:15). The pit is miry (Pss. 40:2; 69:14; cf. 69:2). Jeremiah sinks in it (Ps. 69:2, 14). The case of Jeremiah does not mean that all the references to the pit in the laments should be taken literally. It does mean that such laments would be appropriate at least there. It further suggests how the image could have such force or how language is capable of moving back and forth between literal expression and imaginative power, thus proving itself durable and useful for all sorts of human expressions.

These examples from the psalms and from Jeremiah suggest the possibilities in hearing the situations of those who cry out in the laments against the variety of human experiences, personal and corporate, that come forth from the biblical stories. The resonance between lament and human story may help us give concreteness and content to the plight of the troubled petitioners of these prayers. The interpretive task is not tied to the search for a single explanation for a particular lament but can center in opening up, through different stories and moments, examples of the human plight that may be articulated through the richly figurative but stereotypical language of the laments.

Such an interpretive move receives its strongest confirmation within the Christian tradition by the way in which the Passion stories of the Gospels are related to Psalm 22. Lament and narrative of Jesus' sufferings are bound together. The dividing of Jesus' garments (Mark 15:24; Ps. 22:18); the people deriding Jesus and wagging their heads (Mark 15:29; Ps. 22:7); the words of the people, "He trusts in God; let God deliver him now" (Matt. 27:43; Ps. 22:8); and Jesus' cry of forsakenness (Mark 15:34; Ps. 22:1) all invite one to see in Jesus one of those who cry out in the laments. His plight becomes a paradigm of the trouble of the lamenting petitioner; and his experience of personal agony, of God-forsakenness, and of the taunts and attacks of various kinds of enemies and evildoers gives us the cardinal example of how the dimensions of the lament express the realities of human experience. So the reader of the Gospels is provided Psalm 22 as an interpretive clue to understand who this one on the cross is and what he is undergoing, and the reader of Psalm 22 is invited to see in the passion of Jesus a concrete and specific example of what these laments are all about (see the exposition of Psalm 22 in Part 2).

5. ENTHRONED ON THE PRAISES OF ISRAEL: INTERPRETING THE BIBLICAL HYMNS

While neither the text of Ps. 22:3 nor the translation given in the title above is secure, the Old Testament gives ample testimony to the fact that the glory of God is primarily reflected and declared in the praise of Israel (though not in *Israel*'s praise alone, as we shall see below). The most exuberant, extensive, and expansive indicators of who and what God is, and what God is about, are found and elaborated in the hymns and songs of thanksgiving that the people of Israel and individuals in that community uttered again and again in the course of Israel's history. There the sovereignty of God is given language and structure. There the power and majesty of the Lord are uncovered and made visible. In the hymns of Israel the most elemental structure of Old Testament faith is set forth. So in the praises of this people the foundation stones of both theology and piety in the Judeo-Christian tradition are laid down. In what is said we learn of the one we call Lord. In the way it is said—both shape and tone—we are given a model for our own response to God.

The task of the interpreter, therefore, is less a matter of concretizing the situation and uncovering its correlation with past experiences and present experience, as is the case with the laments, and more a matter of discerning the shape and content of the faith expressed and seeing if our piety can issue in the same doxology. Praise is language to God and about God, elicited out of the human experience of God. What are the central theological claims and themes of the biblical hymns that the interpreter will seek to uncover in the communication of individual hymns as well as the Psalter as a whole?

Form-critical study of the psalms over the past fifty years shows the

64

effort on the part of biblical interpreters to sort out the types and forms of speech characteristic of Israel's positive response to God as distinguished from its petitionary address to God, which is most often found in the lament or complaint psalms (see chap. 1). The results of that study have implications for understanding the theological character and context of Old Testament praise.

One of those results is the point emphasized by Claus Westermann in his ongoing study of the psalms, to wit, that the psalms of praise are genuinely *response*[1] and reflect one pole of the continuum on which human address to God in the psalms is to be placed. That continuum is a movement between supplication and praise, and the basic modes of prayer are to be discerned in the polarity of petition and praise, which in Westermann's analysis are two sides of a single coin. Such a view of the psalms as prayer may seem oversimplified when one looks in detail at the many examples in the Psalter. But there is a fundamental apprehension in this analysis that is on target and consistent in a large way with the data from the psalms. We discern from this model that praise is not one item on a long list of elements that belonged to proper or normative prayer in the Old Testament. It is the very heart of the matter. When Israel, whether corporate or individual, addressed God, the primary mode was either plea for help or praise for God's glory. These are in a sense *the primal forms of speech and of faith.* Nor can they be neatly separated from each other even if they can be distinguished. That is the significance of speaking of a polarity and a continuum rather than simply elements of prayer. Frequently psalms of praise allude to God's response to the situation of distress in the past (e.g., Pss. 8:2; 18:4–19; 34:4–6; 40:1–2; 65:2–3, 5; 66:13–14; 106:44; 107:6 and passim; 124: 1–5; 136:23–24; Exod. 15:1–12, 21; 18:10; Deut. 33:26–29). Even more frequently the numerous lament Psalms allude to or anticipate the praise of God by the one or ones who have been delivered, either by a vow to praise God (Pss. 5:11–12; 7:17; 13:5–6; 22:22–25; 26:12; 31:7) or by a declaration of praise (Pss. 28:6; 31:21; 35:9–10; 36:5–9). The faith of Israel is worked out and articulated on this continuum, a trust in God in every situation, which expresses itself even in the anguished cry for help by one who feels abandoned or even done in by God and also in the joyous shouts of praise of those who have experienced the Lord's grace and goodness and know that God is Lord of all.

A cardinal example of the movement described above may be found

1. Claus Westermann, *Praise and Lament in the Psalms* (Atlanta: John Knox Press, 1981), 122.

in Psalm 107, which demonstrates the richness of Israel's expression of praise and thanksgiving. The growth and composition of this psalm may have taken place in several stages as Walter Beyerlin has suggested,[2] but the final form is a theological whole that I have described elsewhere:

> The Yahwistic community is in the picture from the beginning, and its history and present plight echo throughout the Psalm so that it is always moving on two planes, the individual and the communal, the general and the particular, the existential and the historical. . . . The Psalm in its interaction of form and content is virtually a theological paradigm for the Psalter. It sets forth in its formal structure and repetition the movement from cry for help to divine deliverance to human response of praise. As it moves from strophe to strophe a significant area or metaphor of human need and human fulfillment is set forth: exile (v. 4) → place (v. 7); hunger and thirst → sufficient food and drink; prison → liberation; sickness → healing. This structure is then climaxed by the familiar announcement of Yahweh's turning things around in behalf of the weak, the troubled, the needy. All of this operates on the different planes referred to above and all of it serves to exalt the Lord and make known his power and his way. In its final verse the extended hymn is given us for praise and instruction, to use to magnify the God of whom it speaks and as a guide for our lives.[3]

In thinking about praise of God as one of the primary biblical modes of faith in God and speech to God, one must recognize that the continuum of prayer between supplication and praise is not just a kind of pendulum swing that means the praying Israelite always moved back and forth between petition and praise or that these were in a sense simply the two components of prayer. Rather one always was moving *toward praise*. While the service of worship in the community might *begin* with the praise of God as the people entered the sanctuary and while one would cry out for God's help again in a new situation or distress, the logic of Israel's mode of faithful prayer is clear. Praise and thanks are in a sense the *final* word, the direction one is headed, in the relationship with God. There the expression of faith has moved from a focus on the human situation to reach that end toward which human life has been set, that is, the glorification and praise of God.[4]

2. Walter Beyerlin, *Werden und Wesen des 107 Psalms* (Berlin: Walter de Gruyter, 1979).

3. Review of W. Beyerlin's *Werden und Wesen des 107 Psalms* in *Vetus Testamentum* 32 (1982): 256.

4. A powerful New Testament articulation of this movement toward the glorification of God is seen in the conclusion of the Christ hymn in Phil. 2:5–11, where it is Jesus who is worshiped and praised by all. One finds a later confessional understanding of this goal of human existence in the first question of the Westminster Shorter Catechism, which sees the chief end of human life as "to glorify God and enjoy him forever."

This movement toward praise is not just reflected in individual psalms. Indeed it is found in the very shape of the Psalter, which is dominated in the first half by lament psalms, but moves increasingly to hymns of praise.[5] This movement is by no means a simple, single-line direction. There are hymns in the earlier part, and there are laments toward the end of the Psalter (e.g., 140—143). But the shift of emphasis is noticeable. To go through the Book of Psalms is to be led increasingly toward the praise of God as the final word. While doxology *may* be the beginning word, it *is* clearly the *final* word. That is so *theologically*, because in praise more than in any other human act God is seen and declared to be God in all fullness and glory. That is so *eschatologically*, in that the last word of all is the confession and praise of God by the whole creation. And that is so *for the life of faith*, because praise more than any other act fully expresses utter devotion to God and the loss of self in extravagant exaltation of the transcendent Lord who is the ground of all. The literary arrangement of the Psalter gives clear testimony to this reality as each book of the Psalter is concluded with doxology (Pss. 41:13; 72:18–19; 89:52; 106:48), and the Psalter as a whole ends in Psalm 150 with a call for everything to praise God in every way that is possible. The final word of the Psalter is its climax and anticipates God's ultimate purpose for all creation: "Let everything that breathes praise the Lord" (Ps. 150:6). Even the Hebrew title of the Psalter, *těhillîm*, "hymns," indicates that the primary intention of the book as a whole is to render praise to God.[6]

Outside the Psalter there are other indications of Israel's experience of the continuum of supplication and praise and the movement of faith toward doxology. The heart of the Old Testament story of the people of God is the exodus event recounted in Exodus 1—15. That story is set totally within the movement from the lament of the people under Egyptian slavery and oppression (Exod. 2:23–25; 3:7, 9; 6:5) to the loud and joyous hymns of praise by Moses, Miriam, and the people after God has destroyed the Egyptian army (Exod. 15:1–18, 21).[7] The delivering power of God brings freedom out of bondage, joy out of tears, and leads the community to the realization and declaration of who God is as the incomparable Lord of power and grace. The account of the birth of Sam-

5. Westermann, *Praise and Lament*, 250–58.

6. Cf. J. Reindl, "Weisheitliche Bearbeitung von Psalmen: Ein Beitrag zum Verständnis der Sammlung des Psalters," in *Congress Volume, Vienna 1980*, ed. by John Emerton (Leiden: E. J. Brill, 1981), 339.

7. Walter Brueggemann, "From Hurt to Joy, From Death to Life," *Interpretation* 28 (1974): 14; and Westermann, *Praise and Lament*, 259–65.

uel moves from the anguished, bitter lament of Hannah over her barren-ness (1 Samuel 1) to her exultant hymn of praise to the God who is able to invert the human situation and give a child to the barren one (1 Samuel 2; see below). In Isaiah 40—55 the hymnic praise of the Crea-tor is a response to the lament of those who think God is unwilling or powerless to save (see, e.g., esp. 40:12–31), and the songs of praise in these chapters (42:10–13; 44:23; 45:8; 48:20–21; 49:13; 52:9–10; 54:1–2) generally stand as calls for jubilation at the end of each section of the book, seeking to turn exiled Israel's laments into songs of praise.

That is the purpose of praise—to respond to the experience of God's grace and power, to exalt the one who is seen and known to be that way, and to bear witness to all who hear that God is God. In that sense the praise of God in the Old Testament is always devotion that tells about God, that is, *theology*, and proclamation that seeks to draw others into the circle of those who worship this God, that is, *testimony for con-version*. Indeed no aspect of the Old Testament serves as a vehicle for getting at the biblical notion of God in as full and extended a fashion as do the songs of praise and thanks—and this in part because they point back to the supplications and God's way with the human creature as well as forward to God's intention for the whole creation. Perhaps less clear in the minds of many readers of the Old Testament is the fact that the praise of God is the most prominent and extended formulation of the *universal* and *conversionary* dimension of the theology of the Old Tes-tament. One might even speak of a missionary aim if that did not risk distorting the material by suggesting a program of proselytizing to bring individuals into the visible community of Israel. That is not the case. But what blossoms and flourishes in the New Testament proclamation of the Gospel to convert all persons to discipleship to Jesus Christ is *anticipated* in the Old Testament's proclamation of the goodness (*ṭôb*) and steadfast love (*ḥesed*) of God. That proclamation of goodness and steadfast love is a sure pointer to the one who is the Lord of all life and the only one who can claim the full worship of every creature, a worship that is appropri-ate even on the part of those who themselves may not have consciously experienced the powerful control of their lives by the God of Israel but who hear intimations of it in Israel's praises.[8]

8. It must be stated in clear terms, however, that the New Testament outcome of this Old Testament move toward universal praise is not the only possible direction or outcome. One need not be apologetic about the missionary task that is given the church, to be clear that historically and theologically the Old Testament call for all creatures to praise the Lord can take a different direction.

This character of the songs of praise as proclamation that expresses and evokes praise, seeking to elicit it from everyone and everything that lives and breathes and moves, is seen both in the *form* of the hymn and in its *content*. While a hymn of praise can be elaborated in various ways, its basic structure is clear and consistent. There is either a *declaration of praise* or a *call to praise God* (or both) and a *reason* that is set forth to indicate why praise is appropriate and indeed compelling or unavoidable. The simplest form of the song of praise, that is, the hymn or *těhillāh*, begins with the declaration or call to praise and moves to the ground or reason, as for example, in the oldest hymn of all in Exod. 15:1–18, which is given in its short form in v. 21:

> Sing to the Lord, for he has triumphed gloriously; the horse and his rider he has thrown into the sea.

But the call to praise may be repeated after the reason is given, or before any declaration of praise there may be a statement of what God has done (e.g., in Ps. 40:1–2), though, not surprisingly, this is much less frequent. The primary aim of the song of praise is to set forth or elicit praise, so that aim shapes the song. It is perhaps essential at this point to note that much of the form-critical study of the poetic texts that express the praise of God has focused on the question of whether or not a distinction can be made between praise and thanksgiving. While that particular issue is not the focus of this chapter, it is clear that some such distinction can be made. Gunkel underscored this in his differentiation of the song of thanksgiving, which accompanied sacrifice and expressed thanks to God for the deliverance of an individual from distress, from the hymn, which ascribes praise to God more generally for various (or all) aspects of God's greatness and work. Westermann has recognized this differentiation in his distinction between narrative praise (Gunkel's song of thanksgiving and Hebrew *tôdāh*) and descriptive praise (Gunkel's hymn and Hebrew *těhillāh*) while at the same time insisting— as his technical terminology indicates—that praise and thanksgiving are parts of a single whole, which in the Old Testament must be understood under the rubric of praise, in that the primary aim is to exalt and glorify God while recognizing that such praise virtually always arises out of what God has done and thus is responsive and thankful.

This discussion, to which others have also contributed, is important and has helped us understand better both praise and thanksgiving, however much or little they are differentiated. But from the perspective of Old Testament theology it is important to recognize that the *tôdāh* and *tĕhillāh*, thanksgiving and praise, have come together so thoroughly in the Old Testament that one cannot really sift out one from the other as a legitimately separate theological subject. One has only to look at the easy interchange of verbs and nouns from the roots *ydh* and *hll*, together with other words for singing and rejoicing, to see that these are pieces of a whole. Or one can examine such texts as Chronicles and Ezra-Nehemiah (e.g., 1 Chron. 16:4; 23:30; 29:10–13; 2 Chron. 5:13; 7:3, 6; 20: 21–22; Ezra 3:10–11; Neh. 12:46) to see how *hillēl* and *hôdah*, praise and thanks, are put together and often identified with or defined by each other. This coming together may have happened at a late stage, but its impact is clear throughout and informs the present character and content of the Old Testament. For this reason I assume that praise and thanksgiving belong together and are to be interpreted together as an aspect of Old Testament theology.

The *act* of praise, which in a most basic way is the goal of existence, means to acknowledge and confess who God is and in so doing render honor and glory to the one who is the object of praise. It is at the same time gratitude and thanksgiving because God has shown forth as the God who has demonstrated divine care and providence, a beneficent activity in behalf of individuals and community. Such praise is not, therefore, separated from human experience; nor is it an isolated, abstract activity. The point of the second part of the structure, the *reason* for praise, is to give a rationale for the human adoration. It makes sense. It is a natural and appropriate response. The hymns of praise of Moses and Miriam (Exod. 15), Deborah (Judges 5:3–5), and Hannah (1 Sam. 2:1–10), however composed, are in their spirit and character spontaneous, real, and enthusiastic. Like the psalms of praise and the hymns of Isaiah 40—55, they are also joyous in tone. If one cannot understand the laments of the Old Testament without a sense of the real anguish and despair of heart they convey, it is also the case that one cannot fully comprehend what took place and takes place in praise without feeling the emotions of exultation and delight, shouting and dancing. Praise may even approach ecstasy at times. It is never irrational, however. To the contrary, praise is a making glad that makes sense.[9]

9. The final psalm in the Psalter, Psalm 150, is a clear exception to the otherwise fairly consistent form of songs of praise, i.e., a form that includes a declaration or call to praise plus a reason for praise. Only the call to praise appears in Ps. 150, and in that case is expressed in elaborate, even extravagant, terms. The call to praise is reiterated over and over and, as noted above, broadened to call everything to praise the Lord. The key to understanding the violation of form is found in the placement of this psalm at the end of the Psalter. The whole Psalter and all the preceding hymns have given all the possible reasons

That is true even of those calls to praise that do not seem to arise out of particular or single experiences of God's help but more generally praise the majesty and power and might of the God of creation (e.g., Pss. 19:1–6; 96; 104; 148). Acknowledging the glory of God in such a manner is analogous to the acknowledgment of the beauty of a flower—simply because it is and its beauty elicits from any and all beholders the exclamation of praise and wonder. When one experiences that, praise is real, extravagant, and unavoidable. Indeed the very enjoyment is not fully realized without the expression of praise and wonder. To enjoy God is to glorify God, even as lovers always glorify each other—whether for particular reasons or experiences or simply because of the relationship—both always expecting the glory and praise of the other, but neither giving it only because it is expected.[10]

The Old Testament paradigm of the song of praise is the stanza that one finds at the beginning of Psalm 118 and frequently elsewhere, especially in Chronicles where it is regularly quoted when reference is made to the people and the priests praising or giving thanks (2 Chron. 5:13; 7:3, 6; 20:21; Ezra 3:10–11; Jer. 33:10–11; Pss. 106:1; 107:1; 118:1, 29; 136:1 and passim):

> O give thanks to the Lord, for he is good;
> his steadfast love endures forever.

In this definitive thanksgiving hymn the community declares its fundamental understanding of God, in the reasons it gives for exalting and thanking God.[11] To speak of God as good is to affirm that the Lord of Israel is the source of all that makes life possible and worthwhile. It is an all-encompassing attribute that catches up everything positive that human beings receive in life and often is experienced specifically in God's deliverance of persons from distress.[12] This benevolent and gracious

and motivations for praise of God, and it is not necessary at the end to repeat all that. Psalm 150 functions, in effect, like the final "Hallelujah!" or "Praise the Lord!" that accompanies the various Hallel psalms (e.g., Psalms 111—118). Having called to praise and given reason for praise throughout the psalms, the Psalter now concludes, as do those earlier hymns, with a final straightforward call to praise. This psalm, therefore, is the "Hallelujah!" note for the whole book.

10. See the discussion of praise in C. S. Lewis, *Reflections on the Psalms* (New York: Harcourt, Brace & Co., 1958), 90–98, for a similar analysis of the dynamics of praise.

11. On this common hymn see also Klaus Koch, "Denn seine Güte währet ewiglich," *Evangelische Theologie* 12 (1961): 531–44.

12. Note the summary interpretation given by James L. Mays in his interpretation of Psalm 100, "Worship, World, and Power," *Interpretation* 23 (1969): 327: "In this declaration 'good' designates Yahweh as the one who, within the sphere of relationships to other persons and powers, confirms and sustains and fulfills personal existence." Mays's study is

condescension of the majestic and transcendent Lord in order to save is further acknowledged as the ground of praise and joy in the reference to God's steadfast love (*ḥesed*); *ḥesed* is a term that points to the covenantal faithfulness of God, which has been experienced concretely in the past and is so firmly the basis for Israel's hope and trust that the community can speak of that faithfulness as the content of the future as surely as it knows such a way with God in the past.[13]

In similarly brief scope, Psalm 117 expresses the same theological understanding as this typical hymn of thanks, but it speaks in even stronger terms in declaring that "his steadfast love has prevailed over us" (Ps. 117:2). The psalm testifies that what prevails over "us" is not the enemy but the steadfast love of God. The singers of this song know themselves to be dominated, controlled, overwhelmed by that love.

A comparison of Ps. 118:1–4 and Psalm 117 also highlights the character of praise as a *declarative* act, "telling abroad God's great deeds"[14] to elicit the praise of all. In Psalm 118 Israel and the priests are told to declare that "his steadfast love endures forever." In this act the Lord is praised and testimony is borne, a testimony that is meant to summon all humankind to the praise of God and thus to an acknowledgment and worship of the Lord of Israel. Here is the political and eschatological thrust of Old Testament praise in its insistence that the lordship of this God is universal in scope and should bring forth the conversion of every being to the worship of Israel's God. This call to the nations and peoples to praise the Lord is no incidental or exceptional matter. It is pervasive in the Psalms, where "all the earth" (33:8; 66:1; 96:1; 98:4; 100:1), "the earth" (97:1), "the coastlands" (97:1), "all the inhabitants of the earth" (33:8), "all flesh" (145:21), and "peoples" (47:2; 66:8; 67:4, 5, 6; 148:11; Deut. 32:43) are called to praise and bless the Lord again and again. In Isaiah 40—55 the conversionary character of these songs of praise is explicit (Isa. 45:22–25). The declarative and confessional character of Israel's praise, with its power to evoke the praise of all creatures, is nowhere more clearly laid out, however, than in Ps. 22:22–31, where the singer who has been delivered stands in the midst of the congregation and

an excellent exposition of the theology of praise as exemplified in one of the classic songs of praise. Cf. the reference to God as *agathourgon*, "doing good things" or "bestowing benefits," in the hymnic section of Paul and Barnabas's words at Lystra, rejecting worship of themselves and exalting the living God—an obvious occasion for hymnic or praise speech (Acts 14: 15–18).

13. For a full theological study of the term *ḥesed* in the Old Testament see Katharine Sakenfeld, *Faithfulness in Action: Loyalty in Biblical Perspective* (Philadelphia: Fortress Press, 1985).

14. Westermann, *Praise and Lament*, 77.

tells of the Lord's power (cf. Pss. 35:18; 40:9), that the children of Israel hearing of God's great power and goodness will themselves praise and glorify the Lord. But the power of this testimony does not stop there. Beyond Israel, "all the families of the nations shall worship before you" (v. 27). Yet even that does not exhaust the circle of praise, for those who have died shall praise the Lord (v. 29),[15] as well as generations yet unborn (vv. 30–31).

The scope of such declaration and praise is not, however, confined to human beings and human communities. All the works of God, the whole creation, the heavenly beings, praise God (Pss. 29; 69:34; 97:6; 98:7–8; 148; Isa. 42:10–11; 44:23; 49:13; Joel 2:21–22). They even testify to God's greatness and pass the word on in order that others may hear, praise, and worship (Pss. 19:1–4; 97:6; 145:10–11).[16] The creation that is good (Genesis 1) praises the Creator whose power and glory are reflected in the creation.

For all these reasons the language of praise may be viewed as the speech that is truly primal and universal. All existence is capable of praising God and does so. In such speaking God is identified. Indeed there is very little if anything that comes to expression in the Old Testament revelation of God that is not formulated or echoed in the hymnic and praise speech of Israel and the creation. A full elaboration of the way in which hymnic form and praise language tell who God is and what God does would require a full-scale Old Testament theology, but some of the basic themes can easily be identified.

From beginning to end, one encounters in Israel's praises the conviction that the Lord of Israel is the power behind all that is, creating, shaping, making, fashioning, stretching out, measuring, commanding everything into being. The tendency within the wisdom movement to catalogue and list the elements of the natural order—a tendency that Gerhard von Rad suggested is reflected in the hymnic material of Job 38 and Psalm 148[17]—is at least theologically of a whole with the virtually endless list of God's creative acts in the hymns of praise. Even Genesis 1

15. This is against the view or fear that the dead, being cut off from life, the essential content of which is praise, as well as from the knowledge of God's gracious deeds, cannot therefore praise (Pss. 6:6; 30:9; 88:10–12; 115:17; Isa. 38:18–19).

16. "We encounter the idea that the world is not dumb, that it has a message, in the hymn" (Gerhard von Rad, *Wisdom in Israel* [Nashville: Abingdon Press, 1972], 162).

17. Gerhard von Rad, "Job xxxviii and Ancient Egyptian Wisdom," in his *The Problem of the Hexateuch and Other Essays* (New York: McGraw-Hill, 1966; London: SCM Press, 1984), 281–91. More recently Delbert Hillers has challenged the association of Psalm 148 with Egyptian onomastica in favor of its rootage in ancient Near Eastern hymnic traditions, "A Study of Psalm 148," *Catholic Biblical Quarterly* 40 (1978): 323–34.

seems to be a narrative form of the description of God's creative work. And the elaborate hymnic *listing* of all God's acts of creation in a series of descriptive clauses (e.g., Psalms 104; 136; Isa. 40:12–26; 44:24–28) is echoed in the elaborate mustering of all God's creatures—heavenly and earthly, animate and inanimate—to praise the Lord. The hymnic understanding of the whole cosmos as God's handiwork (Ps. 8:3) and also as God's worshiping audience serves to "de-divinize" totally the natural world so that nature in whatever form is not seen as possessing power beyond God's control, while the praise of the Lord by the whole creation serves implicitly to deny the possibility of other powers as legitimate recipients of praise.[18] In such hymns as Psalms 104 and 147, one discerns Israel's conviction that creation, while it was the first of God's great acts for which praise is due, is not simply a past event but continues in God's preservation of the creating and sustaining of the world and its inhabitants, providing at every moment the matrix and conditions for existence.

It must be recognized, therefore, that the distinction between God as creator and God as Lord of history is more a convenience for the sake of systematizing our theological categories than it is a real distinction. It conforms neither to our modern conceptions of the unity of the divine activity[19] nor to the picture one receives from the Old Testament, where God's activity in creation and history are parts of a whole. The hymnic sections of Isaiah 40—55 affirm the wholeness of God's work in various ways. Isaiah 44:23–28 is a good example as it begins in calling the elements of creation—heaven and earth, mountain and forest—to sing praise because *the Lord has redeemed Israel*. Then in elaborate hymnic form, in a long series of clauses describing God, the creative work of God is described. But along with the clause "who stretched out the heavens alone, who spread out the earth" (v. 24), that series includes "who says of Jerusalem, 'She shall be inhabited,' and of the cities of Judah, 'They shall be built and I will raise up their ruins'" (v. 26); that is, the creative work of God includes the re-creation of Jerusalem and Judah as a home for God's exiled people. In vv. 27–28 the hymnic description of God as the one "who says to the deep, 'Be dry, I will dry up your riv-

18. On the implicit and explicit polemic associated with Israel's praise, see R. Martin-Achard, "A propos de la theologie de l'Ancient Testament," *Theologische Zeitschrift* 35 (1979): 63–71. See also W. Brueggemann, "'Impossibility' and Epistemology in the Faith Tradition of Abraham and Sarah (Gen. 18:1–15)," *Zeitschrift für Alttestamentliche Wissenschaft* 94 (1982): 624–25.

19. On the unity of God's activity see Gordon Kaufman, *God the Problem* (Cambridge: Harvard Univ. Press, 1972), chap. 6.

ers' " is followed immediately by the appositive, "who says to Cyrus, 'My shepherd, he shall fulfill my purpose.' " The one who is able to command the deeps to dry up is the same one who is able to use Cyrus in the divine redemptive purposes (cf. Isa. 45:8).

Two psalms of praise well illustrate the interaction of creation and history, nature and grace, as the single stage upon which the drama of God's one and total purpose is worked out. In Psalm 136 the paradigmatic song of praise and thanksgiving ("O give thanks to the Lord, for he is good; for his steadfast love endures forever") is the basis for a litany of praise that, as it exalts the power of God as witnessed by the people, moves easily through the works of creation into the exodus and conquest events through which God delivered Israel and created it as a people.[20] Then the psalm concludes by praising God for three actions that represent the Lord's saving power in behalf of Israel and God's providing care of all humankind:

> who remembered us in our low estate,
>> for his steadfast love endures forever,
> and rescued us from our foes,
>> for his steadfast love endures forever,
> who gives bread to all flesh,
>> for his steadfast love endures forever.
>> (vv. 23–25)

Psalm 33 elaborates the character and work of God in the context of praise and singing a new song. In vv. 4–5 a series of attributes defines the Lord of Israel in some very basic ways:

> For the word of the Lord is upright;
>> and all his work is done in faithfulness.
> The one who loves righteousness and justice,
>> the steadfast love of the Lord fills the earth.

What is that *word* and *work* that is faithful, righteous, just, and loving? One would expect it to be the Lord saving Israel, delivering the poor. But in a move that is fraught with theological significance, the work and word of God that is just and righteous, faithful and loving is said to be *the creation of the universe* (vv. 6–7).[21] The beginning of the faithful love of God and the justice of God is not an act of deliverance from op-

---

20. The specific language of creation is applied to God's formation of Israel as a people in such songs of praise as Exod. 15:13 ("the people whom you have created"); Pss. 95:6–7; 100:3 (cf. Deut. 32:6).

21. Note the reference to "word of the Lord" and the use of the verb "make" in both v. 4 and v. 6.

pression (though the psalm will go on to include that most clearly in God's faithfulness and steadfast love, in vv. 18–22). It is the beginning of everything. Out of the justice of God the heavens were made. In a not dissimilar fashion the New Testament sees the wholeness and oneness of the work of God in the person and work of Jesus, as, for example, in the Christ hymn of Col. 1:15–20:

> He is the image of the invisible God, the firstborn of all creation; for in him all things were created, in heaven and on earth, visible and invisible . . . all things were created through him and for him. . . . For in him all the fulness of God was pleased to dwell, and through him to reconcile to himself all things, whether on earth or in heaven, making peace by the blood of his cross.

Creation and the reconciliation of creation are worked in the one who is the image of the invisible God and in whom resides the fullness of God.

Insofar as the songs of praise of the Old Testament exalt and make known the Lord of history, they do so primarily through three images, which are themselves parts of a whole and not indicative of discrete aspects of the reality of God. The dominant image is God as *king*, whose rule is manifest over Israel (Exod. 15:18; Deut. 33:5; Pss. 47:6; 99:4; 100:3; 145:1; Isa. 40:10; 43:15; 44:6; 52:7–10), but also, as the enthronement hymns stress, over the gods of heaven (Pss. 29; 89:5–8; 95:3; 96:4–5; 97:7–9) and the nations of the earth (Pss. 47:2, 7–9; 93:1–2; 96:10; 97:1; 99:1; 145:10–13).[22] Indeed the primary explicit declarations of the kingship and sovereignty of the God of Israel are to be found in the hymns of praise, such as Exodus 15; Deut. 33:1–5 and 26–29; the enthronement psalms (Psalms 47, 93, 95—99); and other hymns such as Psalms 29, 145, and 149, as well as Isa. 52:7–10.

Very much related to the image of the king is that of God as *warrior*, for it is by the Lord's victory over the forces of chaos (Pss. 89:10; 93: 1– 4; Job 9:8; 26:12; 38:8–11) and the enemies of Israel (Exod. 15:1–18; Pss. 47:1–4; 48; 98:1–3; Isa. 42:13) that the divine rule is established.[23]

22. The establishment of God as king clearly has its roots in the mythology of the ancient Near East as well as the historical experience of Israel. In the mythopoeic background, the pattern is essentially as follows: *(a)* the combat of a god with the forces of chaos; *(b)* victory; *(c)* building a house as abode for the god; and *(d)* declaration or manifestation of eternal kingship. This pattern comes over into Israel, but three things are emphasized there: (1) The rule of God is centered on human communities (though not exclusively, as indicated above). (2) Temporally and spatially that rule is extended without limits. (3) It is something expected for the future. See F. M. Cross, *Canaanite Myth and Hebrew Epic* (Cambridge: Harvard Univ. Press, 1973), chaps. 5 and 6.

23. The Lord's victory over chaos and over Israel's enemies cannot be as neatly divided as this sentence may suggest. On this see Cross, *Canaanite Myth*, chap. 6. On the whole

Songs declaring the Lord's victory are scattered throughout the hymns of praise as, for example, in Ps. 118:15:

> The sound of glad songs of victory
>   in the tents of the righteous:
> "The right hand of the Lord does valiantly!"

(Cf. v. 14; 48:10; 98:1–2; Isa. 40:10; 52:10.) In a similar fashion those hymns of praise that celebrate the rule of God also speak specifically of God as *judge* (Psalms 96, 97, 98, and 99). Here the hymns identify the character of God's rule as one that enhances and sustains justice and righteousness. At the same time an eschatological dimension to God's rule is underscored as the enthronement hymns particularly anticipate the coming of God to judge the nations, that is, to decide for the right and against the wrong (Pss. 96:13; 98:9).[24]

Finally, no interpretation of the contribution of Israel's hymns of praise to the theology of the Old Testament would be complete without recognition of how these songs declare the radical *transforming* power of God, a power at work in behalf of the weak, the innocent, and the righteous, and against the powerful, the guilty, and the wicked, a power that is capable of reversing reality and the human situation from its existing and expected state into a totally different state. In a variety of ways the hymns of praise exalt the power of God to create a new reality that is in accord with the Lord's just and loving purposes by putting down the mighty and powerful and raising up the lowly and weak (Pss. 75:8; 107:33–42; 113:7–9; 146:9; 147:6; Job 5:11–16; 12:17–25; cf. the proclamation in Isaiah 40—55 of the new thing God is going to do.

Human destiny is not inevitably set. If the status quo is not in accord with God's righteous rule, it can be turned upside down. Nowhere is this more sharply articulated than in the Song of Hannah (1 Sam. 2: 1–10), which from beginning to end exalts God as the one who not only is able to, but does in fact, transform and reverse things as they are. That view of God's reality is echoed in the Magnificat of Mary (Luke 1:46–55), who tells us that God imagines and shapes things in a quite different way from the normal run of things, that the great among the lowly and the lowly among the great is God's way with the world, a way that is

matter of the relation of the imagery of warrior to that of king, see P. D. Miller, Jr., *The Divine Warrior in Early Israel* (Cambridge: Harvard Univ. Press, 1973), esp. 155–65 and 174.

24. On doxology in the context of judgment (e.g., Josh. 7:19; Amos 4:13; 5:8–9; 9:5–6), see J. L. Crenshaw, *Hymnic Affirmation of Divine Justice* (Missoula, Mont.: Scholars Press, 1975), and G. von Rad, "Gerichtsdoxologie," in *Schalom: A. Jepsen zum 70. Geburtstag,* ed. K. H. Bernhardt (Stuttgart: Calwer Verlag, 1971), 28–37.

demonstrated in the story of the birth of Jesus and even more clearly in the events of Jesus' trial, death, and resurrection.

Walter Brueggemann has linked these celebrations of God's transformations with the Old Testament stories of God's wonders (*pĕlā'ôt*, *niplā'ôt*) or "impossibilities which represent a major theological trajectory through the Old Testament that begins in the story of the announcement that Sarah will bear a child and the human reaction of laughter countered by the divine word: 'Is anything impossible (*hăyippalē'*) for the Lord?' (Gen. 18:14)"—a rhetorical question that in Brueggemann's terms bears witness "to a distinctive and radical claim in Israel . . . that conventional definitions of reality do not contain or define what God will yet do in Israel."[25] The hymnody of Israel "continued to speak about the radical freedom of God and the disjunctive character of God's way over, against and distinct from every presumed world"[26] in its praise of the wonders or impossibilities of God's power, beginning with that paradigmatic inversion of power when God put down the powerful king of Egypt and lifted up a powerless oppressed people (Exod. 15:11). Out of Israel's celebration of this impossible transformation, "songs of impossibility" became a constant part of its doxology, whether with reference to the primal impossibilities of Israel's creation (Pss. 78:4, 11, 12; 105:2, 5; 106:7, 22; 136:4), or to God's deliverance of persons in any kind of hopeless situation (Ps. 107:8, 15, 21, 24, 31), or to God's activity generally (Pss. 72:18; 96:3; 98:1; 111:4; 145:5).

Thus the songs of Israel's praise and the form and language of the Old Testament hymnody encompass in the broadest fashion possible the fundamental themes of Israel's faith. All that is God hears the praise of all that is created. The hymns of Israel stand in service of the central theological claim of the Old Testament, that the Lord of Israel alone is God and requires the full devotion of all creation. The expression of praise was the glorification and enjoyment of God, the true measure of piety and the proper purpose of every creature. So for Israel the first and last word of faith was "Hallelujah!"

25. Brueggemann, "'Impossibility' and Epistemology," 622.
26. Ibid.

PART TWO
Exposition of Selected Psalms

PSALM 1

In thinking about the meaning of Psalm 1 and its appropriation, two features should be kept in mind. One is the way the psalm richly illustrates the conception of form and content, the contribution of poetic features to the communication of the word of the text to the reader (see chap. 3 on Ps. 1:1). The second feature is contextual, the fact and significance of the placing of Psalm 1 as an introduction to the Psalter. Attention to both of these dimensions will enrich one's hearing and understanding of this psalm.

STRUCTURE

The poetry of Psalm 1 is reflected not only in the rich parallelism (see chap. 3) but also in the structure and movement of the psalm as a whole and the two similes of the tree and the chaff that stand at the center of the psalm. The movement of the psalm revolves around and demonstrates *the contrast of two ways of life*: the way of the righteous (vv. 1–3) and the way of the wicked (vv. 4–5). The last verse (v. 6) provides the final contrast and a true conclusion in the formal sense (i.e., the psalm comes to an end there) and in the material sense (i.e., the way of the wicked comes to an end). Even within the two parts of the psalm, however, the contrast is made and the psalm constantly sets these two ways off against each other by a number of stylistic features. The righteous one does not "stand" in the way of sinners (v. 1) as the wicked do not "stand" in the judgment or place of judgment. The expression "council of the righteous" (RSV: "congregation of the righteous") in v. 5 is as much a play of words on "counsel of the wicked" (v. 1) in Hebrew as it is in English. The contrast of righteous and wicked is sharply delineated by the two similes of the tree and the chaff at the center of the psalm, which provide a kind of pivot around which the whole swings. The use of these figures of thought in juxtaposition to each other pushes one to compare the two ways, but the character of the two images draws the sharpest of contrasts—the firm, planted, permanent, and productive tree over against the chaff, ephemeral, insubstantial, utterly useless. The difference is even heightened by the varying *lengths* of the similes. The first is detailed and three lines long. Much can be said of the transplanted tree. The second contains a single short relative clause. Of the chaff there is nothing to say except that the wind drives it away to nothingness. That is all there is to chaff.

THE WAY OF THE RIGHTEOUS

The way of life of the righteous is described in three ways: in a statement about what such a one does not do (v. 1), in a description of what is in fact central to the life of the righteous (v. 2), and in a figure of thought to make vivid the way (that is, both the manner and the outcome) that is characteristic of this approach to life. All of this is placed under the rubric "Blessed is the one who . . ." or "How happy is the one who . . .", a phrase that stands outside the parallelism of the rest of the verse.

This blessing formula at the beginning of the psalm sets the tone of the psalm and is echoed at the end of Psalm 2 (see below). The psalm and—by inference from its place at the beginning—the whole Psalter are set to make a primarily positive statement about a mode of life that is ordered to the Lord's way. The expression "blessed," *'ăsrê*, means that under discussion here are not just two ways of conduct but a celebration of a life that takes real pleasure in living according to God's will, that finds itself thus under the care and guidance of God and so is the object of true envy on the part of all who look upon it. The term expresses envious desire. So while the psalm paints a negative result for the wicked who do not follow God's way, its primary aim is to describe the virtues and good outcomes of the way of the righteous whose pleasure in the Lord's law eventuates in and has its corollary in the positive emotional response on the part of those who view him or her. The "way of the righteous" really is a better and more desirable way, and others can perceive and testify to that. The psalms that follow in the Psalter will characterize this way in detail.

The actions rejected by the righteous one while they are described in three parallel cola that emphasize the basic point scored in the first colon of the three (see chap. 3) are essentially two types of conduct: engaging in the kinds of activity that are characteristic of sinners, arrogant scoffers, and evildoers, and associating or consorting with such types. The first action is depicted on the one hand by the verb "go" or "walk," with the connotation of a mode of conduct or way of living, but also in the second colon of the three by one of the most pervasive biblical images: *the way*. The imagery of the way is a powerful figure that conveys a double meaning. The way one goes can have reference to both one's *conduct* and one's *destiny*. In conduct the righteous way is characterized negatively by a refusal to engage in the kinds of activity that are typical of sinners, scoffers, and evildoers, those who are opposed to God's way and threaten the well-being of others in the community, as well as those who are arrogant and scornful and who generally by their words disturb the community and bring distress to others, quarreling and sowing dissension (v. 1). Positively, that righteous way is a constant devotion to the torah of the Lord, that is, to making the Lord's instruction and teaching one's business and pleasure (v. 2). The law of the Lord that is to be found in these psalms and elsewhere is the will of God revealed, a good way for one to go in life. There is no sense here of God's law as a rigid and discouraging burden that cannot be handled. Rather it is the object of one's constant attention, a joy and pleasure that brings about a desirable, indeed enviable, result or reward for the shape of one's life.

The contrast of the ways that Psalm 1 sets up is brought to sharpest expression in the two images of the tree and the chaff (vv. 3–4). The tree is *transplanted*. The one who follows the righteous way is like a tree on a dry plain when it is moved to the water's edge and transplanted. It just takes off, and one is impressed with the rich fruitfulness of such a one. Stability, durability, freshness, productivity—all these things are conveyed by that image. The conduct and destiny of one who constantly delights in the Lord's way is like that. When set alongside the other way that ignores and perverts God's instruction, the difference is obvious: the firm, planted, and productive tree over against the unstable waste of chaff. There is nothing to it. Nor would one ever choose or envy the dead chaff in preference to the rich, living, transplanted tree.

While this psalm, like so many, has no explicit historical setting to which it should be assigned or restricted, its language and concerns echo the opening chapter of Joshua (1:7–8) in a way that is suggestive and illustrative. In that chapter the Lord commissions Joshua to take his place and passes on to him the leadership of the people, as they go in to settle the land of Canaan. The Lord's words sound almost like a quotation or pastiche from Psalm 1 (or vice versa):

> Only be strong and very courageous, being careful to do according to all the law which Moses my servant commanded you; turn not from it to the right hand or to the left, that you may have good success wherever you go. This book of the law shall not depart out of your mouth, but you shall meditate on it day and night, that you may be careful to do according to all that is written in it; for then you shall make your way prosperous, and then you shall have good success.

The way set forth in Psalm 1 is given as the way for the leader of the people at the beginning of this new stage of their existence and as the only way for the one who leads God's people to endure in the face of many difficulties that lie ahead and to be confident of successful completion of the task that lies ahead. The wisdom that one finds in Psalm 1 is thus seen to be instruction for a Joshua and, by inference, those who follow in his train as leaders of the community of faith. Whatever handbooks may be generally useful, the primary direction for the leader is found in God's instruction as it is read, studied, heard, and absorbed into one's being as a constant guide. It is no accident that the only word to the king in the whole Deuteronomic law is an instruction to him to write down a copy of this law, God's instruction to the people, and keep it with him as a daily guide, reading and studying it and being very careful to follow it constantly. We find here a clue to the reason that the psalm begins speaking of the righteous as an individual even though it eventually uses the term collectively (v. 6). One at least is able thereby to envision a Joshua, a Deborah, a David or a Paul finding in these words helpful and right instruction for his or her role as a leader, even as the words suggest the centrality of devotion to the Lord's instruction as a characteristic of other and later leaders of the community of faith.

The psalm concludes with the claim that the Lord "knows" one of these two ways, the righteous, but the other way, the way of the wicked will perish (v. 6). It is a simple and straightforward statement, made by those who knew that life was not always perfect and full of rich rewards for those who sought to be obedient to God's way and that some who followed another way seemed to get along well enough. So why and how is such a claim put forth without any qualification? We cannot say with any certainty, but we can at least pay close attention to what the text says as we hear it in the context of the whole of Scripture.

"God knows the way of the righteous" is to declare that the Lord takes notice of and has regard for the way that those who are righteous go. That way is not hidden from God or a matter of indifference. It is under God's oversight. As Calvin readily recognized in his commentary on this psalm, there may be no outward advantage to a life marked by right conduct and attention to the Lord's instruction, but it is marked by God in the sense that God takes note of such a life as well as in the sense that God marks the way for such a life so that persons of such bent are known to God and kept in God's care. What that means concretely for the vicissitudes and trials of life's journey or the manifestation of leadership and guidance of the community of faith is quite open-ended and unspecified, as necessarily must be the case, but the claim and wisdom of this psalm is that, all along, the way is undergirded and tended by the Lord.

There is a certain ambiguity here in that the text does not say specifically what God does, an ambiguity that is extended in the claim of the second colon that the way of the wicked perishes. Here there is no word of divine action or agency but simply the declaration that a way marked by evil and immoral conduct, disdain for God's instruction and will, cannot be ultimately sustained. It finally dies. Like chaff it is insubstantial waste and goes with the wind. While there are many biblical hints of God's judgment upon those who go such a way, in this psalm one senses that it is almost in the nature of things that the wicked way goes under. That may be affirmed in an eschatological sense and surely is in the proclamation of the death and resurrection of Jesus. The evil way is finally done in. But this psalm suggests to us—and bids us open our eyes to look for the evidence—that in a more proximate sense wickedness often does itself in and leads to its own destruction in a world that is shaped and governed by God's moral order. Whether it is a matter of the evil way sowing the seeds of its own destruction, or of human effort to overcome the forces and manifestations of wickedness in the world, or of God's righteous work to maintain the divine purpose against efforts to subvert and obstruct it, the result is the same according to the wisdom of Psalm 1. The wicked way as a mode of *conduct* contrary to God's instruction and to God's way is real in this world; but the way of the wicked as a *destiny* and *outcome* will not endure.

In summary then, to hear Psalm 1 as it is given to the community of faith, that is, as an introduction to what follows in the rest of the Psalter, is to be pointed down a particular path, a way that will be elaborated and unfolded in the psalms that follow. That way is described in negatives, that is, as avoidance of a style of life characterized primarily by consorting with or taking counsel of those whose moral actions are reprehensible, aligning oneself with the arrogant, those who scoff at and deride obedience to the Lord. The righteous way is also spelled out in positives centering in the joy and delight of constant devotion to the Lord's instruction. The negative words and the positive words are obviously two sides of the same coin. This law that becomes both business and pleasure is not life-killing or an unbearable burden but a joyous word of God's grace and God's call.

There are positive effects and results for the followers of this right way that should not be glossed over. They are expressed in the word of approbation "blessed," the vigorous fertile tree, and the knowledge or care of the Lord. Whoever follows this right way is judged to have hold of something good. Such a one who drinks from this well, plants her or his roots in this deep stream, is invigorated and fruitful, in some sense clearly prospers, indeed experiences God's care. The chaff-like fate of the life of dissolution, oppression, and immorality is widely to be seen without building it into a fixed order or knowing altogether what that fate is.

In the rest of the psalms we hear a great deal about people who act and speak like the wicked, the sinners, and the scoffers of this psalm, the pain they inflict, and the cries of those who suffer by their words and deeds. But we hear also of the joys of that unceasing attention to the Lord's teaching and the positive effects and results for the righteous one who walks by that teaching. The placing of this psalm as the introduction to the Psalter serves to lift up the role of the whole collection of psalms as a book of instruction for true piety and ethics and not just a book of liturgy for the worship of the community of faith.

The way that is opened up in this first psalm, however, leads not only into the psalms that follow but far beyond them. One hears its echoes in the frequent "blessed" of the beatitudes of Jesus, where the happy state is still connected to following the Lord's instruction and law (Matt. 5:17–20) and where joy and reward are found but not necessarily apart from persecution and suffering. We hear the way pointed out to us again in the words of one who says to us, "I am the way," and who in his own way with others and in his journey to the cross defines for us even more clearly and sharply the way of the righteous one. It is well for us to remember that precisely for this reason those who are now called Christians were first called "those of the Way" (Acts 9:2; cf. 19:9, 23; 22:4; 24:22). If we would still bear that title, then it might be well to sing the psalms as we go. They will help point us in the right(eous) direction.

The introduction to the Psalter does not conclude with Psalm 1. It carries over to the second Psalm, as is immediately evident by the absence of a superscription at the beginning of Psalm 2 to mark it off from Psalm 1, as well as by the presence of a concluding "Blessed . . ." clause at the end of Psalm 2, which echoes the "Blessed . . ." clause at the beginning of Psalm 1 and forms a poetic bracket or envelope around both psalms in a way that shows them to be a two part introduction to all that follows.

But now the ground has shifted and we do not hear about the individual who follows God's righteous way. Rather we hear the tumult of nations in league, as powerfully articulated in Leonard Bernstein's musical expression of this Psalm in his "Chichester Psalms" (see the exposition of Psalm 23). The world of kings and empires is in view, not the modes of personal and moral conduct, the individual piety of which Psalm 1 speaks. The shift, however, may not be as radical as appears at first glance but may be more one of emphasis. For here also, as we noted above, there is a concern for identifying the kind of existence or conduct that evokes a judgment of approbation and envy by those who perceive it, a judgment that such a one and such a way are "blessed" (Ps. 2:12). Furthermore, there is a similar conclusion that warns of a way that does not endure; and God's knowing the way that is directed by the law or instruction of the Lord (Psalm 1) is balanced in Psalm 2 by God's wrath kindled against those who set themselves against the Lord's rule and purpose.

So there is a resonance between these two psalms that helps us hold them together as an introduction to the Psalter. Still the shift of emphasis and shift of scene in Psalm 2 is important and demands our attention to its particular concerns and instruction.

If one reads through Psalm 2 several times it is difficult to miss its very dramatic character. The clash of conflict rings through the psalm. The dramatis personae are the protagonists in this conflict: on the one hand, nations and peoples together with their rulers; on the other hand, the Lord together with the Lord's anointed. The speaking voices change and vary in the course of the psalm. There is movement and action. The psalm is lively and confrontational.

The setting of the drama may be seen from two perspectives. From one angle the stage is the whole cosmos—the kings and nations on earth, the Lord sitting enthroned in heaven, the Lord's anointed on Zion, which is politically the capital of Judah and religiously the earthly abode where the Lord has caused the divine name to dwell as manifestation of God's presence and rule. From another perspective and more specifically, the human and social setting of the psalm is an occasion of enthronement or coronation of a Judean king and the possible or actual revolt of vassals at the time of accession of a new king. Such transition times were not infrequently regarded as periods of weakness when subordinate rulers could move away from or against the nation ruling over them because of the absence of a strong and experienced ruler in control. Josiah's territorial and religious moves when Sinsharishkin succeeded Ashurbanapal on the Assyrian throne is a good example, but such rebellions and testings are a part of power politics and the interplay of nations in their struggle for hegemony and autonomy in any period. That is why the human setting, remote though it may actually be, resonates with any time nations and rulers struggle for control and power or to break free of that. From either perspective, therefore, the issue is world power, and the affairs of the small state of Judah are claimed to be of universal and cosmic scope. The fundamental and deepest question addressed by the psalm is whether the disorders of history are an indication that the forces of chaos still control, and whirl is king, or whether there is a power ruling in the cosmos that can bring order out of disorder and overcome the inevitably self-seeking and ultimately tyrannous character of all human powers.

The plot or action of this particular drama is the gathering together and secret scheming and plotting of the kings and nations against the Lord and the Lord's anointed with the purpose of throwing off their rule and control. The not too well hidden and audacious presupposition of the psalm is that the tiny kingdom of Judah in southern Palestine and its king and God could claim ultimate power over all the nations and kings of the earth. One might reasonably expect such claims from the capitals of Assyria, Babylonia, or Egypt; but despite all the apparent evidence to the contrary, the psalmist, together with the people of Judah as they carried out the coronation ceremonies, persisted in declaring that such a claim belonged to its king and God alone. While the realities of world politics of the day must have presented an unceasing challenge to the claim, Judah persisted in boldly setting it forth whenever a new king ascended the throne.

The first act or scene of this drama is set on earth and tells of the plotting of the human rulers (vv. 1–3). The one who speaks is the psalmist, the offstage narrator of the drama, who before the psalm is over moves on stage to address the rulers. The question "Why do the nations conspire and the peoples plot in vain?" is not a complaint but a derisive challenge that represents a biblical analysis of the problem on the plane of world history. The critical words or phrases of this scene are two:

Against the Lord and his anointed (v. 2c). The Psalm is not talking generally about international treaties and alliances but the resistance to the ultimate rule of the Lord as manifest through the Lord's agent. One will have difficulty searching for an actual time when such control and rule by the Lord of Israel through the king of Israel was apparent, but one will find that this people never stopped asserting the reality of such rule, especially in the royal psalms..

> May he have dominion from sea to sea,
>   and from the River to the ends of the earth!
> May his foes bow down before him,
>   and his enemies lick the dust!
> May the kings of Tarshish and of the isles
>   render him tribute,
>   may the kings of Sheba and Seba bring gifts!
> May all kings fall down before him,
>   all nations serve him!
>
> Ps. 72:8–11

Plot in vain (v. 1b). The word for "plot" is the same as the word for "meditating" on the Lord's instruction in Psalm 1. So these two introductory psalms set over against each other a quiet and continuous devotion to the teaching of the Lord as the way of righteousness and blessing in contrast to a vain and empty scheming against God's righteous rule.

The second act shifts the scene to heaven, and the ones who speak are the Lord and the Lord's anointed (vv. 4–9). This act tells of the reaction of the one enthroned in the heavens to the kings, the ones enthroned on earth. The response is twofold. In a marvelous piece of anthropomorphic imagery the narrator speaks of the loud and derisive laughter of God challenging the pretensions of human power (v. 4). The divine laughter is a vivid pointer to the sovereignty of God and the Lord's invulnerability to all human machinations, even those of the most powerful. In a strange way it is one of the most assuring sounds of the whole Psalter as it relativizes even the largest of human claims for ultimate control over the affairs of peoples and nations. The fiercest terror is made the object of laughter and derision and thus is rendered impotent to frighten those who hear the laughter of God in the background.

Then—and the conjunction is explicit in the text and ominous, marking a shift in the action—from derisive laughter the Lord moves in anger against those who would reject the Lord's rule and direction of history (v. 5). The angry word that troubles and terrifies the nations is the anointing of the Lord's agent, the king, and the announcement of his power against the king's position, authority, and power rest totally in and are derived from the Lord: "*I* have set *my* king on Zion, *my* holy hill . . . I have begotton you . . . I will make the nations your heritage" (vv. 6–8). In an official decree the king is adopted as God's son, the very child of God. The divine word "You are my son; today I have begotten you" creates a new existence, identifies this one as the chosen bearer of the rule of the Creator. The nations are given to this ruler as an inheritance to an heir. Power to break them in two should they seek to cast off the Lord's rule is given to the chosen ruler.[1] The power of this ruler is real, but it is not characterized by oppressive tyranny. It is the Lord's righteous way (see the exposition of Psalm 1). Psalm 72 again gives us a clue to the nature of this anointed one's rule:

> Give the king thy justice, O God,
>   and thy righteousness to the royal son!
> May he judge thy people with righteousness,
>   and thy poor with justice!
> Let the mountains bear prosperity for the people,
>   and the hills in righteousness!
> May he defend the cause of the poor of the people,

---

1. Verse 9 is more properly translated, "You *may* break them. . . ." See J. A. Emerton, "The Translation of the Verbs in the Imperfect in Psalm II.9," *Journal of Theological Studies* 29 (1978): 499–503.

give deliverance to the needy,
and crush the oppressor.

(Psalm 72:1–4)

God's rule through the Lord's anointed is a reign of justice and righteousness, security and well-being, and resistance to oppression (cf. Isa.
9:6–7; 11:1–5). The dominion of the anointed one over the kings and
rulers of the earth is not an exchange of one tyranny for another. It is the
creation of God's kingdom, a human community not left on its own or
potentially victim to whatever strong forces seek to control and domi-
nate others, but rather truly shepherded and secured by God's rule
through the human ruler.

The final act of Psalm 2 returns to earth and Zion with the prophetic
word to the kings and nations who conspire (vv. 10–12). The logical
conclusion to draw from the decree and the empowering of the king is
instruction and warning. The fear of the Lord is the beginning of wisdom, and to such fear the rulers of earth are enjoined. Such wisdom also
involves submission to the universal dominion of the Lord's anointed, a
dominion that brooks no separate or independent claims to power. It is
clear at the end. The Lord, through the anointed one, reigns over all.
Happy are all who find their refuge in the Lord (v. 12c).

So as the introduction to the Psalter comes to a close we learn that this
book will speak to us of individuals and their way and destiny but also
of kings and nations and their conduct and fate. The righteous one before the law of the Lord and the rulers before the anointed of the Lord
are both in view. The modes and questions of individual conduct and
the behavior of peoples and nations are matters of concern in these
psalms. In the move from Psalm 1 to Psalm 2 the human plane is greatly
expanded. If we have moved from a way the individual should walk to
the rule of nations and empires, it is still the way of the Lord and the
Lord's rule. And Psalm 1 may be a word of instruction to the king or
other rulers and leaders even as Psalm 2 is a word of assurance to the individual member of the community of faith. So the reader of the Psalter
is led to understand that it speaks about individual piety and ethics and
also about the larger horizon of world affairs, foreign policy, human
government, and international alliances, about the rule of God over nations and parliaments, kings and presidents, as well as the individual
life of faith. The way of the Lord's instruction and the rule of the Lord's
anointed are the chief clues to what matters in all of this.

In this psalm, then, the historical and political realities of Israel's history, its life under a monarchy, become the vehicle for a vivid and dramatic assertion of the sovereignty of God, a sovereignty that is manifested and carried out through those agents who are chosen to be the bearers of God's rule, and wrought out in the conflicts and power struggles of human history. The psalm understands that the divine politics is a genuine synergism, that there is one who is called into special relationship to the Lord, to carry out God's rule and to receive the gift of a universal dominion. But that rule and that dominion are never an end in themselves. The consequence or end result of establishing the Lord's anointed as king is to bring all other kings and all nations to the service and worship of the God of Israel. The world rule of the Lord's king means the world's worship of the Lord.

Israel saw in its parade of kings the struggle for power enacted but the final result never accomplished. It did not, however, relinquish the vision of the Lord's rule in history carried out through one who was chosen by God, a righteous and just king, victorious for God, judging the poor with equity, providing blessing for the people, bringing the nations into the worship and service of God.

Many still look for such a king. Some who inherit this vision have given it up as utopian or simply fruitless. Others claim to have discovered that king in the midst of our history, the one who has brought into being the righteous rule of God, Jesus of Nazareth. They have seen the fulfillment of this announcement of the begotten Son (Acts 13:33; Heb. 1:5). They have seen him beset by the nations and powers of this world. They understand him to be the king, the one whose kingship is in behalf of the Great King, whose rule in our midst always points to a larger dimension.

But if this psalm helps us both look for and perceive the Lord's anointed as well as know what it is he is about, it is also the case that Jesus and what the New Testament tells us about him define afresh for us the nature of his power and the shape of his rule. The confrontation between Jesus and Pilate in John 18 is an illustration of that deeper understanding that Jesus gives us into the reign and power of God. There the critical issue is the right understanding of the kingship of Christ. Indeed from the appearance of Jesus before Pilate to his death on the cross, the claim of Jesus' kingship is the ongoing theme.

What sort of king is it, however, who wears a crown of thorns and manifests his kingship on a cross instead of a throne? That is the problem Pilate never resolved; so he assumed that Caesar, one of the kings of the earth, was in charge. The kingship of Jesus turns out not to be like any human kingship. He does not manifest his rule in earthly power and glory but in the giving up of himself in behalf of a sinful and suffering humanity. His power over the world is precisely his powerlessness before the world, the laughter and anger of God that have the strange shape of tears. As he took all that the world (the kings and peoples) could give, he died in its behalf and broke the power of anyone or anything else that would claim total control over our lives.

This means that the kingship of Christ is real but not obvious. Nowhere is that more surely demonstrated than in the crucifixion. The title Pilate ordered for the cross was meant to be a mockery: "The King of the Jews"! The crucifixion should have shown without a doubt that this was no king or, if so, no power to contend with the absolute rule of Caesar. Yet Pilate's action in fact bore witness to the truth he claimed not to perceive, and ironically the first homage to Jesus as a king was made by those who crucified him. Pilate thought to have taken care of the troublesome Nazarene, that he would cause no more trouble to Rome. On the surface he had. Little did he know, however; for in the years ahead followers of this executed one would go to prison and the lions because they refused to worship the Roman emperor and acknowledge his kingship over their lives. And eventually the emperor himself would worship this cross-enthroned king and acknowledge his lordship.

Thus it is that the kingship of Christ calls all other kingships into question and places them under the lordship of Christ. In every sphere of life Christ is the one who has ultimate rule over us. His kingship sets us free from the fear of all lesser lords whom we may serve obediently and even willingly, who may cause us trouble and suffering but who do not ultimately rule over us. The anointed of God alone claims and exercises that lordship. That is the message of Psalm 2.

"The fool thinks there is no God."

PSALM 14

"First one must note the remarkable fact that the existence of deity is never questioned in the Old Testament. . . . There were no atheists in ancient Israel, not even down to the latest times."[1] Thus begins the discussion of the existence of God in a standard and good treatment of the Old Testament understanding of God. Not surprisingly the author refers in this context to Psalm 14, which is found in an alternate form as Psalm 53, and its opening statement: "The fool says in his heart, 'There is no God,'" or better, "The fool thinks there is no God." That is certainly the word in this psalm that most immediately—and lastingly—catches one's attention as the psalm is read, heard, or studied. Nor can one avoid asking if we find any clue here to whether or not the issue of God's existence was present in any form in the biblical word or the mind of the biblical writers. In one sense the dictum I have quoted above is correct, but if one probes more deeply into this psalm and listens to other voices that resonate with it, the issue may be a little more complex than that.

The word about the fool's hidden assumption that there is no God is not merely an introduction to the psalm. It is the controlling theme of the psalm as indicated by its poetic structure and content. Several features identify this as the dominating motif:

1. The lead verse of a psalm often sets up the primary subject matter, as, e.g., in Pss. 1:1; 8:1; 23:1; 42:1; 46:1; 67:2; 90:1; 97:1; 118:1; 121:1; 127:1; 133:1.

1. Robert Dentan, *The Knowledge of God in Ancient Israel* (New York: Seabury Press, 1968), 129.

94

2. The expression "there is no God" is echoed and played on in vv. 2 and 3 and in the expression, *"there is none* that does good."* The poet sets these two reverberating against each other so that by their similarity in the initial "there is not," *'ên,* the reader is led to associate these two sentences in sound and begin to think about how they may relate to each other. And indeed the interaction between the two sentences is where the psalm has a bite and the question about God comes to focus (see below). The resonance of these expressions and the radical nature of the situation is reinforced by the final colon of v. 3, "no, not one," or more literally, *"there is not* ['ên] even one."* The repeated indications of widespread corruption also bind vv. 1–3 together and underscore the point made at the end of v. 3.

3. The clause "to see if *there are* any that act wisely" is a counterpoint to *"there is no* God/no one doing good."* The human situation that the psalmist sees is characterized by "there is not," *'ên;* the situation God (and the psalmist) seek is characterized by "there are," *yēš.* Again the reader is led by the language of the psalm to juxtapose and contrast the world as it is, that is, the absence of God (according to the fool) and of any doer of good, with the world as it should be, that is, the presence of wise people who do good and right.

4. Verses 4–7, with their focus on the oppression of the poor by "evildoers," only appear to move away from the subject of vv. 1–3. As a matter of fact, v. 4 serves to make more explicit the problem that is present in the opening line of the psalm, and then vv. 5–6 give the response of faith to the all too real (and not merely theoretical) issues about both God's existence and human existence that have been raised very forcefully by the psalm.

How, then, are these issues raised by Psalm 14? To begin with the thought of the fool, it must be acknowledged that at one level it does not contradict the statement that "the existence of deity is never questioned." The expression "there is no God" is not an ontological statement denying the reality or "being" of God. It means rather that God is not here or God is not present. As if one were to reach into one's pocketbook and exclaim, "There is no money" or "I have no money." Or if one were to look into the pantry and say, "There is no food." In these cases one does not mean to say that money and food do not exist, but that one does not have any food or money. There is no money or food here.

We need to press further, however, to understand what is happening in this psalm. For it is usually pointed out that even the kind of denial we have in v. 1 appears as the way of thinking of a fool, which indicates at the very beginning of the psalm that it is to be understood as a rejection of such a foolish claim. And indeed the psalm does stand as a counter to that notion. But we must not hear the claim of faith over against the fool too quickly. Why, in fact, is such a statement seen as the thinking of a fool? For one thing, the psalmist does regard the person who thinks this way as foolish precisely because he or she lives and operates on the secret supposition that God is not. That is deemed foolishness. But "the fool" means something else in this psalm. The contrast between "fool" and "wise" (v. 2) is really another way of speaking of the evil person and the good person, the wicked and the righteous. That is confirmed for us by Psalm 10, which is the one other place where the claim is made that there is no God (v. 4), and which generally expresses the same point of view as Psalm 14. There it is the *wicked* who thinks that God is not. Again, of course, the notion is to be rejected by those who are wise and righteous.

The two psalms, however, do not simply report the hidden assumption of people who are wicked-foolish. They go on in some detail to explain *why* such a point of view is taken up, and in their doing so, faith begins to betray its own questions on the way to living by trust in God. It is clear why the foolish one or the wicked one says that there is no God. It is because there is total corruption and abomination, only evil and injustice. The fool or wicked one is a part of that company of corrupt persons who do abominable deeds, who eat up my people like bread, as the psalmist puts it in language reminiscent of Mic. 3:1–4, who oppress the orphan, the widow, and the poor, that is, the weaker and powerless members of the community. In the situation depicted by Psalm 14 the Lord vainly looks for a wise person, defined here as someone who seeks after God, an idea surely to be understood in the context of the prophetic word, where seeking God is not necessarily going to church, prayer, and the like. The fool was probably often "in church." His or her denial of God was quiet, in the mind and heart. Amos, however, directly equates seeking God with hating evil, loving good, and establishing justice in the gate or the court (Amos 5:4–6, 7, 10–11, 14–15). What Amos in effect says is, If you would seek God, make sure that the courts work fairly to ensure justice, that the weaker and poorer members of the community are not that way because of your overly high fees and rents, that you do not become rich and powerful off the poverty and powerlessness of others.

What, then, is the connection between all that and the denial of God? Why does the fool make his or her assumption and live and act as if there is no God? The connection is in the juxtaposition of "no good one" (vv. 1b and 3) and "no God" (v. 1). The very actions of the wicked and the foolish are the strongest evidence against God. They do all their abominable, immoral, and unrighteous deeds; they devour the people— and they get away with it! Psalm 10 spells this out in more detail and takes us deeper into the inner thoughts of the foolish-wicked—and the innocent victim:

> The hapless is crushed, sinks down, and falls
>   by his [the wicked's] might,
> thinking: "God has forgotten,
>   has hidden his face and will never see it."
> Arise, O Lord; O God, lift up your hand;
>   do not forget the wicked.
> Why does the wicked renounce God and think:
>   "You will not call to account"?
>
>   (vv. 10–13)

When the fool or wicked secretly thinks, "There is no God," what he or she means is indeed *God is not here,* God is nowhere around. And what such ones ultimately or really mean is, God is not anywhere around because we can do whatever wicked or unrighteous thing to other people that we choose to do and get away with it. God is far off and uninvolved in the human situation, or God is powerless or unwilling to prevail over against the wickedness that is everywhere apparent. God will not call us to account for our wickedness, our oppression, even the ones who are the Lord's own. In other words, what the fool or wicked thinks is, Whatever may be said or confessed about God, what I see is that God does not make a single bit of difference in the human situation; the wicked go unpunished, the oppressed and weak go unhelped.

What I think one discerns in listening closely to the psalm is that the question about God or the assumption of no God, that God is gone, dead, irrelevant, was very real in Israel. It was an authentic question or claim on the part of the wicked, who worked it out empirically. They found themselves able to carry out their evil and oppressive deeds with impunity. But one misses a very important dimension in the psalm, if one assumes that this claim and the evidence for the claim are made and seen only by the foolish and wicked ones who do not know better. For one thing Psalms 10 and 14 are both lament psalms or variations on the typical lament form. To that extent they function in part to give voice to a genuine despair and anguish before God in the face of oppression and injustice. The assertions of vv. 1–3 describe a situation of total corrup-

tion, absolute evil. The statements, "They are corrupt, they do abominable deeds, there is none that does good—they have all gone astray, they
are all alike corrupt; there is none that does good, no, not one!" are the
words of one who has looked out on the world and seen only darkness,
that inhumanity and despair that raise the question about God in the
most elemental fashion. But that view of the human situation is articulated *by the psalmist of faith.* The evidence that leads the fool or the unrighteous to the God-denying conclusion, to wit, a hopeless situation where
evil runs rampant and there is no sign of the presence of God and no resistance to the total evil that would suggest the presence and involvement of God, is starkly real and deeply felt by the psalmist also. So the
question about God is raised also, implicitly, on the part of believers
who uttered a lament in the face of the evidence and asked a genuine
question: Where is God? The issue in that theistic question, as I have already suggested, is whether or not God is present in the human situation and whether or not God is able or willing to do anything about it. It
is at base the question of whether or not God makes any difference at all.
Now that is not the same thing as an ontological denial of God, but I
would argue that this is the only form in which the theistic question has
any bite at all and is, in fact, usually where people find themselves in
deepest doubt about the existence of God. If God is not present in the
human situation, and if God is not powerful and manifests no power to
redeem the human situation, then does any claim about the existence of
God have any meaning or reality at all?

I am suggesting, therefore, that the theodicy questions, the questions
about God's reality, power, and goodness, were present implicitly in the
midst of the believing community and barely underneath the surface in
many of their laments. That is not a matter of indifference to the contemporary community that joins with the psalms and seeks to gain some
theological direction from them. For the fourteenth Psalm ends up in a
ringing declaration of faith. The psalmist dares to claim in the midst of
the God-denying facts all around that God is indeed present with the innocent sufferers and victims ("the generation of the righteous"—RSV)
and that those who would oppress the poor and devour God's people
will find themselves shattered against the refuge that God provides. But
if the questions that belong to our faith and doubt in conversation with
one another and to our experience in the modern world have no point of
contact with questions uttered by the community of faith long ago, then
it may be difficult for us to take with much seriousness the answers and
directions they give us. If, however, there is a significant resonance be-

tween our theological questions and fears and those of the ones who long ago wrote and prayed these psalms, then it is appropriate and meaningful for us not only to join in singing the psalms with them but also to pay attention to their claims of faith in the midst of doubt and despair.

There is, of course, no final proof that faith is legitimate in the darkness of our life. In the gospel one piece of evidence is given us to confirm that God is present with the weak and oppressed, to comfort and to deliver. That evidence is the life, death, and resurrection of Jesus Christ. In him the fullness of God was pleased to be present in our midst. He was born among the poor, his birth celebrated by poor shepherds. His ministry was among and to the poor, the weak, the sick, the oppressed, and indeed even to the rich and powerful. He gave them his loving care and ministered to their needs. His presence was God's presence, his compassion God's compassion, and finally one who was a member of the "generation of the righteous" was devoured at the hands of the corrupt, the wicked, the evildoers, and thus he confirmed forever the faithful conviction of the psalmist that God is present with the oppressed and at work to overcome oppression.

One cannot know the why of all the greater and lesser terrors of our human pilgrimage that continually call in question the reality of God, the presence and power of the Lord. We dare to hope, with the psalmist, that the crucified one is present even in the darkest of such terrors, that Immanuel is the clue to the heart of all reality.

"My God, my God, why hast thou forsaken me?"

PSALM 22

The theological significance of Psalm 22 commands the attention of any interpreter of the psalms. Not only is it in some ways the individual lament par excellence but it also provides the chief interpretive clue to the Passion of Jesus in the Synoptic Gospels (see the conclusion of chap. 4). Psalm 22 is picked up over and over again by way of quotation, allusion, or indirect influence in the New Testament portrayal of the death of Jesus and the events surrounding that occasion. In line with the interpretive proposals of chapter 4, the Gospel narratives offer a context for making visible and concrete the cries and images of Psalm 22. In this case, however, the New Testament narratives offer more than illustration. The interaction of Psalm 22 and the passion narratives helps us understand what both are about in a way that might be less clear if we viewed the subject matter of each without reference to the other. Indeed, that has often been the case with regard to the story of Jesus' death and resurrection, and the theological results are very noticeable (see below). In these pages we want to hear the power and meaning of this lament as a psalm of one in trouble and then ask further what it tells us about the central event of the Christian revelation.[1]

If one may call any psalm a typical lament, this one would surely qual-

1. Some very helpful articles for understanding this psalm are provided in *Interpretation* 38 (January, 1974), particularly John Reumann, "Psalm 22 at the Cross: Lament and Thanksgiving for Jesus Christ," 39–58; and Claus Westermann, "The Role of the Lament in the Theology of the Old Testament," 20–38 (*Praise and Lament in the Psalms* [Atlanta: John Knox Press, 1981], 259–280). My exposition is greatly influenced by both these studies. An important treatment of this psalm that appeared after this book was in press is James L. Mays, "Prayer and Christology: Psalm 22 as Perspective on the Passion," *Theology Today* 42 (1985): 322–31.

ify. In it one finds the basic characteristics of the Old Testament complaint or lament of an individual: address to God, complaints, petitions,
the certainty of a hearing, and a final song of thanksgiving. The three
parties that regularly (not always) show up in lament psalms—God, the
individual, and the enemies—are all here. In some ways the most obvious feature of this psalm is its *movement*, a shifting back and forth from
complaint to expressions of trust but clearly in a slowly ascending move
from the deepest depths of vv. 1–2 to the most extravagant thanksgiving and praise in vv. 22–31. On the way to that height there is a genuine
struggle of the soul that finally moves from utter hopelessness to the
conviction that God has heard and responded to the anguished cries of
this human sufferer.

Ps. 22:1–5. The depth of anguish as well as the very real tension in the
relationship of a trusting believer who feels abandoned by God is sig-
naled in the very opening line of the psalm. The repeated "My God, my
God," is unusual in the laments, a clue to the intensity of the cry in this
case. Equally significant is the pronoun, "*My* God." In the deepest despair, in a situation where all evidence speaks against any claim on a relationship, the psalmist holds to it, presupposes it, and indeed seems to
stake everything on it. From one perspective the utterance "*My* God"
seems totally out of accord with the complaint that follows. The fact that
it is there, however, lets us know that not only does the psalmist hold to
the covenantal relationship, but it is the only thing on which to hold in
the black darkness that has flooded over.

The question why is not uncommon in laments (e.g., Pss. 10:1; 42:10;
43:2; 44:24, 25; 74:1, 11; 88:15). It is a critical question, the theodicy question, the human question in the midst of suffering. Why, God? The
psalmist gives vent to the sense of *abandonment* by God (cf. Lam 5:20, Isa.
49:14). The why may be a question seeking answers and thus a reflection
of the psalmist's sense of innocence. But it is as much a protest, a complaint, as it is a query (cf. Abraham's question to God in Gen. 15:2,
which is more complaint than inquiry). The question of this sentence
stands in a strong tension with the repeated address. Together they en-
capsulate the whole character of this psalm, which revolves around the
tension between despair and trust, doubt and faith.

In the second colon of v. 1 the psalmist speaks of the *distance* of God,
who does not hear the cries of this suffering one or does not respond:
"Why are you so far from helping me, from the words of my groaning?"
"Groaning" (RSV) understates the Hebrew expression. It is the language

used of the roaring of a lion, and we hear it elsewhere in reference to complaints (Pss. 32:3; 38:9; Job 3:24). The reader hears not simply moans but the desperate, even angry, outcry of the sufferer.

The tension of the first verse is heard again in v. 2: "O my God, I cry by day, but you do not answer." The theme of the verse is the silence of God, an unbroken silence, day and night. Surely as these opening verses give vent to a sense of the *abandonment* of God, the *distance* or *absence* of God, and the *silence* of God, we hear the voice of human suffering at its lowest point and know that the question about God, about the presence and power of God (cf. the exposition of Psalm 14), is not a modern creation but belongs to the very nature of creaturely, human existence. Is the human predicament, however it is experienced, large or small, by one or by many, a testimony to the absence of God from the world and human life? Psalm 22 suggests that at least is how it is felt and perceived.

Out of the depths the psalmist now moves (back?) to affirmations of trust in vv. 3–5. That the issue of trust is the central concern of the verses is immediately apparent from the threefold use of the verb "trusted" in vv. 4–5. The subject matter is the trust in God by the community in the past, a trust that was authentic and well grounded in the Lord's delivering mercy. Reference to the past serves two purposes. It is first of all a part of that struggle of the suffering self who is utterly undone and yet is able to remember that God has not forsaken in the past, that the cries of God's faithful ones (and sometimes the unfaithful ones) have not gone out into the empty void but have been truly heard and heeded. Whatever the present reality, the psalmist knows a larger story, that others have been in this situation in the past, have cried out in pain and anguish, and God has responded. The despair of the soul, terrible as it is seen to be in vv. 1–2, is not the only reality for the suffering one who belongs to the community of faith. The trust of those of the past is a basis and ground for trust on the part of the present one. That does not mean that trust and crying out in pain for help, even crying out in complaint against God, are incompatible. The parallelism of vv. 4–5 is instructive as it suggests that trust and outcry are identical. The sequence of parallel verbs in these verses is, trusted/trusted/cried/trusted. The context reveals that to cry out to God is possible because of the trust in God and the trustworthiness of God. Indeed trust in the Lord is manifest in the cry to God in questioning, seeking, anguish. The interplay of these two verbs, "trust" and "cry out," in vv. 4–5 is a kind of parallelism of the movement of the whole psalm, back and forth from outcry to assertions of trust, indicating that they are parts of a single whole.

Reference to trust of the community in the past and God's response, however, serves another purpose. It is there also as a part of the psalmist's overall plea to motivate and urge God's response to the present plight of the one who suffers and prays. The one who has answered the cries of the people in the past—for illustration see Exod. 3:7–8 and 9–12—will surely answer the present cry of an oppressed individual now. Such expressions that seem intended to motivate and urge God's response and action are fairly common in the lament psalms. They tend to cut against the grain of contemporary notions and practices of prayer. With our sense of the consistency of God's action, our resistance to any ideas of whimsicality in the divine intention that makes God's will dependent upon how urgently we press God, and our dependence upon the model of Christ—"Not my will but thine be done"—we properly hesitate to affirm the validity of such motivating and urging exclamations in prayer. There is, however, some legitimacy to these kinds of words and some connections with our own understanding of prayer. For one thing they assume a theological perspective that is fairly widespread in the Old Testament,[2] that is, that God's purpose and action are involved with and affected by the purposes and actions of those whom God has created. God is independent of human control but has chosen to be responsive to the human situation. There is a kind of openness, a room for maneuvering, not just a willingness but an intention on God's part to be accessible to and responsive to the creation without being dependent upon it and controlled by it. This openness does not introduce whimsicality, capriciousness, and inconsistency into the divine activity; nor do the motivational sentences of the psalmists seek such. It is necessary to recognize—and these verses illustrate the point beautifully—that in the laments the psalmists are urging God to act according to what is in fact God's will and purpose. It is precisely because God's way and manner in the past have been discerned to be merciful to the suffering and delivering of the oppressed that the psalmist can know it is right to cry out in the present. The petitions and the motivational expressions are consistent with what God has revealed about the divine nature. So the psalmist's prayer and urgings are in fact that the will of God be done. They are an urging that God act as God.

Ps. 22:6–11. The conclusion to v. 5 provides the transition to what follows, though "transition" is a mild word to express the emotional char-

---

2. On this see T. Fretheim, *The Suffering of God: An Old Testament Perspective* (Philadelphia: Fortress Press, 1983).

acter of this movement. The translation "they were not disappointed" (RSV) is a little mild if not misleading. Some translations more accurately read the verb *bôš* as "they were not put to shame." For here we encounter one of the primary feelings of those in trouble, a sense of shame at their situation, their powerlessness, and the sense of rejection by God and others. That final word of v. 5 poetically—and probably actually —is a trigger, setting off the lament once more and plunging the psalmist back into despair. The fathers were not ashamed, because God delivered. The psalmist in the midst of unrelieved suffering is covered with shame. An implicit contrast between the present situation and that of the fathers and mothers of the past is drawn, and an actual reversion to the anguish and sense of shame of the suffering one takes place as the psalmist bursts forth with the words of vv. 6–8.

With an emphatic "But as for *me* . . . " the contrast between the present experience of shame and God's past deliverance is now made explicit, and the psalmist adds to a sense of abandonment and helplessness a strong word of low self-esteem and self-loathing, apparently a characteristic of those who feel done in and overwhelmed by forces outside themselves. In the divine oracle of salvation to the despairing and hopeless exiles in Isa. 41:14–16 God addresses Israel as "worm," not a term of endearment but God's recognition of how in fact the exiles saw themselves. Psalm 22 at this point draws together the sense of divine rejection (vv. 1–2) and the sense of self-rejection (vv. 6–8) and in so doing uncovers in its movement a basic feature of human life when it is experienced as overwhelming, depressing, and hopeless. The experience of interaction with other selves and the incapacity to change one's situation create a sense of worthlessness and helplessness—of being helpless to do anything about one's situation and without help from the one source that should always be reliable. Indeed the scorn of those around reminds this despairing petitioner of his or her relationship to God and the apparent uselessness of that trust in God. Before the psalm is finally over, self-affirmation out of divine confirmation and deliverance will ring out loud and clear, but not before this soul has gone through the valley of the shadow and the "Slough of Despond" on a journey through the darkness where no light can be seen.

The jeers of the people (vv. 7–8), however, ironically testify to the truth of the psalmist's relationship with God, and recollecting them, this one is reminded afresh of the care of God that has been a personal reality from the very beginning. And so the psalmist shifts back once again from despair to a self-reminder and a reminder to God that there has been no part of this one's life that has not been upheld by the everlasting arms ("But *you* are the one," v. 9). The experience of life as a gift and the protecting providence of God as all-encompassing from the very moment of birth and felt in the warmth of a mother's breast provide a basis for renewed expression of trust (vv. 9–10). The affirmation "You have been *my God*" (v. 10) echoes the cry of v. 1, "*My God, my God,* why have you forsaken me?" and grounds the apparent contradiction of that sentence in a lifelong relationship with the Lord that existed as the experience of divine care even before the psalmist knew it.

And so the petition comes forth: "Be not far from me" (v. 11). It is rooted in the lament (v. 1) "Why are you so far from helping me?" The plight of the psalmist is stated succinctly: God is far off; trouble is close at hand; there is no one to help. In simple sentences the psalm bears testimony to the human question about God (cf. the exposition of Psalm 14): Is God present in the life of those who trust in God, and can or does God act to overcome the trouble that human beings encounter? The question is never asked outside the experience of trust and some awareness of the fruitfulness of that experience. Indeed it is that history of trustworthiness that turns the earlier question (v. 1) into the present petition (v. 11). The awareness of God's nearness in the past (vv. 9–10) is the ground for the present plea to God to be present and to help.

Ps. 22:12–21. This journey into the darkness is not over, however. Psalm 22 does not recount a momentary scare that is quickly alleviated. The one who speaks in these words is thoroughly done in, beset by powers that are overwhelming. What those powers are the psalm never tells us. The language is specific and vivid, but it is also metaphorical and open. Two images are used: ravenous animals closing in on their prey, and the physical agony of sickness. The former may represent human enemies or oppressors; it may be an allusion to those who mock and scorn. But other possibilities are present also. Parallel expressions in ancient Near Eastern incantations raise the possibility that these beasts are a way of speaking of demonic powers who are perceived as the cause of sickness and suffering. The imagery of the wasted, dried out body may in fact point us to a terrible, deadly illness. But here also that is not the only experience such language can communicate. The psychosomatic character of much illness reminds us of the interplay of external and internal physical distress. Thus the imagery of physical disintegration experienced by one near death is as appropriate for persons whose anguish may be grief over the death of a beloved child, like David's terrible grief over a rebellious but beloved Absalom, as it is for a sick Hezekiah or a Jeremiah beset by family, friends, and the power of the king (see chap. 4). The varied imagery of the surrounding beasts with their mouths open, the evildoers gloating and scoffing, and the body wasting away would all be poetic and powerful expressions for a Hannah beset by a vexing, gloating Peninnah and weeping at Shiloh and refusing to eat because she was barren (see chap. 4), or for a Naboth done in by a kangaroo court set up by Ahab and Jezebel to get his property (1 Kings 21), or for exiles in Babylon, weeping for Jerusalem and taunted by their captors (Isa. 41:8–16; Psalm 137).

So the language is open and inviting. Or perhaps it is available and accessible to those who in any time find themselves in such straits. Indeed it may be that only such poetic images as these have the power to give expression to the primal scream of pain that arises in the human cry to God. One should not miss in the midst of these verses that the psalmist expresses not only a sense of disintegration from within and oppression from those around but also a clear sense that in some fashion God is also involved in the present plight and has done in the psalmist. At the end of v. 15 comes the cry "You have cast me to the dust of death." The singular form of the verb in contrast to the plural verbs in the surrounding verses makes it clear that this is an accusation directed at God. The psalm at this point gives vent to, and allows the troubled one to express, the sense that God is at fault. We do not know what reality lay behind such an accusation. One may hear in these words the voice of one under judgment who knows that to be real—compare Celia Coplestone's sense of sin and the need to atone for it in T. S. Eliot's *The Cocktail Party*—or the echo of a Job who has not heard the dialogue between God and the adversary in the heavenly council but knows that ultimately God is involved in his being cast to the dust of death. Or this may be an anger at God arising out of a sense of the incompatibility between the believed compasion of God and the experienced descent into darkness with no one near to help and only silence from God's corner.

And so the cry goes up once more to that corner: Be present to me in my trouble and give aid to extricate me from it. Then, finally, at the deepest point in the pit an answer is heard:

> Save me from the mouth of the lion,
>   you have answered me from the horns
>   of the wild oxen.
>   (v. 21; see RSV footnote to v. 21)

How this answer comes and what the shape of the response was we do not know. It has been suggested quite plausibly that the psalmist was in the sanctuary and received through the priest an oracle of salvation from God, such as one finds in Isa. 41:8–13 and 14–16 or Jer. 15:19–21. But the psalms give us few concrete clues about this. From what we know of such oracles and from the present context three things may be said:

1. The manner of God's response is often not spelled out except in a kind of imagery that matches the imagery of the complaint. Examples may be seen in Isa. 41:11–12 and 15–16a. So the experience of God's "answer" is as open to the variety of human experience as is the situation that is described in the laments.

2. The translation of v. 21b given above, which is a straightforward translation of the Hebrew text, suggests that in the case of the psalm the response of God comes in the midst of and in some way from the terrible situation itself. The meaning of that is elusive, but the sentence is thought-provoking as it suggests that the response of God is not discerned necessarily in or by or from the experience of extrication out of distress. On the contrary it may be that the comfort and help of God is heard out of the terror itself. In the darkness and out of the oppression one may finally hear what one has sought for (v. 2), the answer of God.

3. Insofar as we can give any content to that answer from what we see in the oracles of salvation, it is directly what has been sought (see vv. 11 and 19): the confirmation of the relationship and its reality experienced as the presence of God with the sufferer in the midst of the trouble and darkness, together with God's promise of help and deliverance from the trouble. Such a word announces a transformation of one's predicament and in its very announcement effects or begins to effect such transformation (note, for example, Hannah's changed countenance in 1 Samuel 1). The dramatic power and effect of such a turnaround is given testimony in the rest of the psalm.

Ps. 22:22–31. The psalm comes to its conclusion—and one might say in some sense its climax—in one of the most effusive and extravagant songs of thanksgiving in the Old Testament. The psalmist reiterates the claim that God has heard and responded (v. 24). As the cry of the fathers and mothers in the past was heard, so God has heeded the present cry of an afflicted one. The psalmist seems to want to counter all the earlier assumptions (vv. 1–2) in v. 24: God has not ignored or disdained the suffering one (v. 24a); God has not "forsaken me" or turned away (v. 24b); God does answer (v. 24b). The affirmation that God is present and

involved is just as strong as the cries of despair. One cannot take the latter any less seriously than the former. Here is one who genuinely experiences God's transforming and delivering power, and it is as real as the
sense of hopelessness and death were.

In this thanksgiving song there are two kinds of movement that are
clues to what it is about. One of these is a movement back and forth between *praise* (vv. 22–23, 25–26, 27, 29–31a) and *reason for praise* (vv. 24,
28, 31b). The other movement is the creation of a *widening circle of praise*.
At the center is the petitioner whose prayer for help has been answered.
This one's testimony to God's power is proclaimed in the midst of the
community, which is called to join in that praise. What had been vowed
in crisis (cf. Ps. 116:17–18) is now paid. Sacrifices are brought, a meal
prepared, and the people partake. But the circle does not end with the
psalmist's own group. The testimony extends to the ends of the earth (v.
27) and shall evoke the worship and praise of everyone (cf. chap. 5).
While the text of v. 29 is not altogether clear, it appears to refer to the
exalted of the earth and even those who are dying or have died. The
mighty and the dying and dead shall join the chorus of praise. Even
generations yet unborn (v. 30) shall worship this God when they hear of
God's response to the sufferer of this psalm.

The double movement of this song of thanksgiving has two effects. It
brings the singers of the psalm from the deepest depths to the highest
heights as it closes with a crescendo of praise to the God who is present
to deliver. There is a movement outwards, however, as well as upwards
as a great ripple, yea a wave of praise, spins out from God's deliverance
of this one person. The praise of the lamenting petitioner is public praise
and can and should elicit an astonishingly wide echo of praise (cf. Ps.
117:1). The utterly desolate and isolated individual who felt a worm,
nothing, mocked by everybody, has moved to the center of a universal
circle of praise and worship of the Lord. The constant struggle between
despair and trust has ended in the dominance of trust, vindicated by the
answer of God.

PSALM 22 AND THE MEANING
OF JESUS' DEATH

It is clearly not sufficient to stop with an exposition of Psalm 22 as an
expression of that primal outcry of human suffering that we hear in the
Old Testament and in our own experience. For in the New Testament
this psalm, which is in many ways the lament par excellence of the Old

Testament, provides the primary interpretive clues to the meaning of the Passion and death of Christ. In the Gospels, Psalm 22 is picked up over and over again, by way of quotation, allusion, or influence, with reference to the death of Jesus and the events surrounding his death, and thus becomes a hermeneutical guide to help us understand what those events mean.

Preeminent in this appropriation of Psalm 22 is the cry from the cross, "My God, my God, why have you forsaken me?" (Matt. 27:46; Mark 15:34), which, as we have seen in the context of vv. 2–3, is a terrible and anguished cry out of the human experience of God-forsakenness, God distant and absent, the silence of God. There is no denial of that experience to Jesus of Nazareth. Where in the Old Testament the human situation of degradation and desolation—a sense of abandonment by God, of being mocked and scorned by everyone—is most strongly attested, the New Testament explicitly identifies that experience as Jesus'.[3] Confirming this understanding are the allusions to the jeers and scorn that are found in vv. 7–8 and echoed in the mockery and taunts of the chief priests, scribes, and elders, and those who passed by Jesus on the cross (Matt. 27:39–44; Mark 15:29–32; Luke 23:35–37), and the allusion to dividing the garments of the lamenter, in Ps. 22:18 (Matt. 27:35; Mark 15:24; Luke 23:34; John 19:23–24).[4]

All of this is very important for understanding the meaning of the death of Jesus. While Christian theology, at least in western Christendom, has largely understood the work of God in Christ's death as God's dealing with the problem of human sin, a point that is developed at length by Paul, the use of Psalm 22 in interpreting Jesus' death points in another direction without necessarily invalidating Paul's understanding. As we read the Gospels we see the deeper meaning of the incarnation in God's identification with all those who suffer and cry out to God. At least one fundamental meaning of the death and resurrection is that it is God's way of dealing with and overcoming human suffering. No more than we can explain atonement can we understand from human

3. While it is proper and important, as suggested here, to keep in mind the whole psalm, including the final hymn of praise, as an interpretive guide to understanding the crucifixion and resurrection as they are presented in Matthew and Mark, and to a lesser degree Luke, one cannot then play down the force of v. 1 by denying to Jesus the experience of anguish and despair that they clearly represent even in a context of trust and on the way to deliverance and praise (so, e.g., Shusaku Endo, *A Life of Jesus* [New York: Paulist Press, 1978], 148–49, 171).

4. For a more extended discussion of the use of Psalm 22 in the New Testament, see Reumann, "Psalm 22 at the Cross."

eyes how this is so. But the Gospels make clear that human pain as well as human sin is in view in the redemptive work of God in Christ.

In a valuable treatment of this subject Claus Westermann has pointed out that

> both in Christian dogmatics and in Christian worship suffering as opposed to sin has receded far into the background: Jesus Christ's work of salvation has to do with the forgiveness of sins and with eternal life; it does not deal, however, with ending human suffering. . . . The impression thus given is that although Jesus of Nazareth actively cared for those who suffered and took pity on those who mourned, the crucified and resurrected Lord in contrast was concerned with sin and not at all with suffering.[5]

The point Westermann is making is cogent. An overly Pauline-oriented theology has understood the work of Christ in a one-sided manner, not taking seriously either the implications of the story of the Passion's being told in terms of the lament of Psalm 22 or the relationship of the death and resurrection of Jesus to the ministry of Jesus. The active ministry of Jesus clearly had to do with human suffering. Jesus of Nazareth heard and accepted the lament of the people around him and acted to deliver them from their particular experiences of suffering. While forgiveness of sins was also a central part of Jesus' ministry and often took place in the context of healing, it did not happen in place of healing. Now one should properly assume a continuity between the intention of Jesus and his active ministry and the intention of God in the death and resurrection of Jesus. The explication of that event in terms of the twenty-second Psalm indicates that the Gospel writers saw Jesus as taking up the lament of those who suffer and entering into that suffering. Jesus Christ died for human hurt as well as human sin. The resurrection is God's response to the cry of the sufferer, the vindication of life over death, the demonstration of God's presence in suffering and power over it. It is not an end to suffering, the continuing existence of which plagues and perturbs us. It does tell us that God is at cross-purposes with suffering, fully present in it, and at work to overcome it. The cruciform character of life is everywhere apparent. The resurrecting work of God is more difficult to see. It did not begin in Jesus Christ nor end there. But its final victory is clarified and sealed in him.

The power of that event to evoke an unending ripple of praise is as clear from subsequent history as it is from the song of thanksgiving in

---

5. Westermann, "The Role of the Lament," 33.

Psalm 22. As men and women of all nations and across all generations have heard the story of God's presence and power in the resurrection of God's suffering one, they have come to know that all the cries of pain have broken through the silence and darkness into the very heart of God, there to be taken up and heeded. Generations yet unborn, the mighty and lowly, the very ends of the earth praise the Lord and proclaim God's deliverance.

"The Lord is my shepherd, I shall not want."

PSALM 23

The most familiar and beloved of all the psalms, Psalm 23, is an open and accessible text, a song of trust in God that has been the vehicle for personal confession of faith and reassurance down through the centuries. Its tone and main themes come through with force and power apart from the necessity of critical reflection. As they do, however, the reader understands the words of assurance and feels their calming tone. The restful waters, the green pasture, the secure path, the quiet, undisturbed fold, all come to life in the reading and hearing of this psalm. One does not need to have much familiarity with the life or work of a shepherd to feel the power of the imagery of this psalm. It speaks to deep human need, even for those whose personal experience has no point of contact with the images presented. The task of the interpreter is thus enhanced by the text's accessibility. At the same time the very familiarity of the psalm presents a challenge to bring it alive so that even, if not especially, those who know it well may not pass it by too quickly but will find themselves drawn afresh by its words into the safe fold of God.

Psalm 23 is one of those texts whose poetic images are the primary vehicle for its mood and content (see chap. 3 and the exposition of Psalm 1). In this case they are images of God, positive images that reinforce the constant claim of the Old Testament that God is the refuge, the rock, the supporting arms, of those who trust in the Lord, and the provider of the rich blessings of life. The first part of the psalm (vv. 1–4) conveys the divine character with the picture of the *Lord as shepherd*, the dominant image of the psalm. The connotations of the metaphor are provided by its use in Scripture and by its context. One encounters the picture of God as shepherd primarily in relation to the people as a whole, particularly in other psalms, such as 95:7 and 100:3, which speak of the community, those who sing these songs, as "the people of his pasture," those guided by God's hand, and also in texts that tell of God's delivering and guiding captive Israel out of exile. The two strongest expressions of this theme are in Isa. 40:11 and Ezek. 34:11–16. The former is one of the most beautiful passages of the Old Testament:

> He will feed his flock like a shepherd,
>   gather the lambs in his arms,
>   carry them in his bosom,
>   and lead those that are with young
>   to a resting place.

In one image the prophet points to God's provision of sustenance for life, the Lord's safe direction, and especially the gentle care that the Lord of the universe manifests toward the small and the weak. It is this portrayal of God's character that is the primary picture the Scriptures give, Old Testament as well as New. Ezekiel 34:11–16 rings the changes on the shepherding heart of God as it depicts the Lord seeking out the strayed and lost sheep, bringing them home to their true pasture, and binding up their wounds.

All of this echoes out of the simple statement of faith that opens and controls the psalm: "The Lord is my shepherd." It is a word of faith, indeed a very basic confession of faith, not in a doctrinal sense, but that experiential affirmation of trust that is rooted in a deep realization *that* one has been cared for and *who* it is that has watched over. While the imagery of the divine shepherd keeping the flock comes to expression primarily in relation to the community led into the promised land in the exodus (Exod. 15:13) or back into that land from exile (see above), in this psalm as in the very nature of the shepherding imagery the individual person is in view as the recipient of God's protecting and providing care. This is not a communal credo. It is the song of trust of someone who knows in the midst of the vicissitudes of her or his personal life and over the course of the years that he or she has been carried in the bosom of God, sheltered from harm, and given rest. That is why the psalm has had such a central place in personal piety and the devotional life.

The corollary of knowing God as one's shepherd is given in the following sentences: "I shall not want," or "I do not lack." The absolute use of the verb *hāsar*, "to want, lack" — that is, the verb used without any object such as food, help, or just anything—is unusual. Indeed it occurs only one other time, in Neh. 9:21, in reference to Israel's experience of God's care in the wilderness: "Forty years you sustained them in the wilderness, and they did not lack." God's provision in the wilderness is an excellent illustration of the scope of this claim. That was for the people a lifetime experienced in the most difficult and uncertain circumstances, when they did not know where they were going or what trouble lay ahead, and when God protected them against enemies and provided food and drink to sustain their life, protecting them as a bird protects its young (Exod. 19:4b; Deut. 32:10–11), as a parent supports a child (Deut. 1:31), or, as in this case, as a shepherd cares for each member of the flock. The claim "I do not lack" is comprehensive, all-inclusive. With the Lord as shepherd, nothing is lacking for life.

Verses 2–4 spell out the claim of v. 1 in vivid detail. In v. 2 the psalmist points to two dimensions of the Lord's provision. The green pastures and still waters image the divine blessing of food and drink to sustain life. But the act of lying down is also a symbol of peace and tranquillity (Isa. 11:6–7; 14:30; Jer. 33:12; Ezek. 34:14–15) and frequently carries with it the additional claim "and none shall make them afraid" (Job 11:19; Isa. 17:2; Zeph. 3:13; cf. Mic. 4:4).[1] So the psalmist evokes in the reader's mind feelings of security as well as sustenance through the peaceful, rich imagery of animals grazing and resting in a verdant watered meadow, to which they have been safely led by their shepherd.

The *effect* of the provision by the shepherd is indicated in v. 3a—refreshment and renewal. The appropriateness of Psalm 23 as a song of trust of one who has cried out to God in time of trouble and been delivered is seen when this affirmation is compared with the lament in Lam. 1:11 and 16, where twice the plight of the exiles is described as needing physical (v. 11) and spiritual (v. 16) restoration and revival. The psalmist has experienced that renewal of vitality that comes from the Lord's provision.

Both the act and its purpose as described in v. 3b are important to the image of the divine shepherd:

> He leads me in right paths
>   for his name's sake.

The main clause is ambiguous. Not only may the prepositional phrase be translated "in paths of righteousness," but the activity of God here

---

1. David N. Freedman, "The Twenty-third Psalm," in *Michigan Oriental Studies in Honor of George C. Cameron*, ed. L. I. Orlin (Ann Arbor: Univ. of Michigan Press, 1976), 150.

may be understood as either leading the psalmist to walk in the way of justice and righteousness (cf. Prov. 2:9; 4:11)—a meaning that would be especially appropriate if the one who speaks were originally the king —or leading the trusting one to walk in safe and correct paths where no harm will befall (cf. Pss. 5:9; 16:11). The latter understanding fits the context, but the former cannot be ruled out, especially if the psalmist has in mind the course of life and not just one particular crisis. Rather than being a problem, the ambiguity may belong to the richness of the psalm and thus need no resolution in favor of one meaning over another.

The psalmist sees in God's guidance a manifestation of the divine purpose. The expression "for your name's sake" evinces the believer's recognition that all this loving care and provision is in keeping with the character of God as one who is compassionate and forgiving (Exod. 22:27b), whose intention in the creation of the world and its inhabitants is blessing of every sort for all people (Gen. 12:1–3), and who is faithful to the covenant. While the activity of God described here is in behalf of the good possibilities of human life, the psalmist does not forget the theocentric character of the universe. It is out of God's character and for God's just and loving purposes, that is, "for your name's sake," that right paths are set for the human journey.

The fourth verse of the psalm is the gospel kernel of the Old Testament, that good news that turns tears of anguish and fear into shouts of joy, that glad tidings given by the angelic choir to the shepherds, which itself echoes a word first given to the patriarchs and repeated again and again to Israel in moments of distress and fear: You don't have to be afraid. This is the salvation word par excellence of Scripture, Old Testament as well as New. The psalmist has heard that word, probably in the midst of threat and danger, and life is now controlled by it. This assurance of the Lord's deliverance in the face of death, in the deepest shadows of existence, is grounded in two realities. One is a confidence in the relationship with God, a conviction that whatever happens the companioning presence of God is there. The promise of Immanu-el, God with us, which is the principal meaning of the incarnation, placarded in the very name of the child of Mary and uttered as his last words to the disciples, "Lo I am with you always," is for the psalmist the experienced reality that takes away all fear. The other reality that disperses gloom is a confidence that God will deliver, embodied again in the promised one whose name is Jesus, "He will save," and expressed by the psalmist in the imagery of the rod, a club for beating off any animals or persons that threaten the flock, and the staff, with which the shepherd reaches out and pulls back any of the flock that start to wander off. This protecting power and presence of God is the ground of all assurance, the alleviation of the deepest fears.[2]

The second part of the psalm shifts images now to portray the Lord as host, who richly provides for the one who sings the psalm. The reference to preparing a table has its closest parallel in the query of the rebellious generation in the wilderness: "Can God prepare a table in the wilderness?" (Ps. 78:19). Here as elsewhere, therefore, we see the poet evoking the rich provision of God in the wilderness experience. D. N. Freedman has aptly explained the impact of exodus and wilderness-wandering themes on the thought and modes of expression in Psalm 23:

> [T]he poet wishes to evoke the past, especially the wilderness experience, but not to dwell on it. His main interest is elsewhere, to use the past as a key to the present and the future, and to express his conviction that the God who was shepherd to his people in the ancient past and led them through the wilderness to freedom, and security, and peace, would and will do the same and more for his people now and in the future. The message is conveyed by an individual to other individuals: each member of the community is a bearer of the tradition, a recipient of the blessing and the promise which inhere in it.[3]

The "presence of my enemies" reminds us again of the possible situation of threat and crisis that may lie behind this psalm. That note is to be heard against the joyous affirmation,

> Surely goodness and mercy shall
>   follow [Heb., pursue] me
>   all the days of my life.

The pursuit of enemies who hound the psalmist trying to do him or her in is a familiar theme of the lament psalms, for example, 7:5; 69:26; 71:11; 109:16; 119:86; and 142:6. But now the one formerly pursued by enemies is chased and pursued by something altogether different—the goodness of God, which is the rich blessing bestowed by God over all of life, and the steadfast love or mercy of God, that unceasing love that is grace and salvation, "help in need," to use Katharine Sakenfeld's summary ex-

2. On the oracle of salvation, which underlies this verse, see Claus Westermann, *Isaiah 40—66* (Philadelphia: Westminster Press, 1969), 11–13. As the lamenter cries out in distress, "There is none to comfort me" (Lam. 1:17, 21; cf. vv. 9, 16), so the one who has known God's presence and help is continually "comforted" by the divine shepherd (cf. Isa. 40:1).

3. Freedman, "The Twenty-third Psalm," 160.

pression.[4] It is no accident that the psalmist finds the whole of life shadowed by good and mercy or steadfast love. These are the primary divine characteristics that are the reason for praise of God. The paradigm of praise in the Old Testament so identifies the grounds for joy and thanksgiving (see chap. 5):

> O give thanks to the Lord,
>   for he is *good*;
>   for his *steadfast love* endures forever.

In light, therefore, of the rich provision of God, symbolized in v. 5 by the anointing with costly oil and the overflowing cup (from my earliest childhood I can remember my mother in moments of deep joy and satisfaction exclaiming, "My cup runneth over!"), the psalmist knows himself or herself to be rooted and grounded in love, chased and overwhelmed by the goodness of God through the whole of life. If this imagery of the Lord as host at a rich banquet reflects at all a thanksgiving meal (see below), then v. 6 represents the psalmist's hope and anticipation of returning and dwelling in the house of the Lord. The theme of continually abiding in God's house is a constant note in the psalms, for example, 27:4-6; 36:7-9; 52:8-9; 61:4. Whether or not the house or tent of the Lord is specifically the sanctuary, the expressed intent and desire at the conclusion of the psalm is to remain always in the sphere of God's presence and deliverance. There is the only security that really holds, and nothing more is needed.

One should not close one's consideration of the psalm without taking account of its association with various contexts that may sharpen its focus or illumine its meaning. One of these is the possibility, if not the likelihood, that the psalm had an original setting in practices of worship, more specifically, the occasion of a thanksgiving meal offered by a person in gratitude to God and fulfillment of vows made in seeking God's help. What the crisis of need was we can never know, though it may have been the plea for help by a person wrongfully accused of a crime, followed by a banquet or celebration after acquittal. The chief clues to such a connection with a thanksgiving meal are in the reference to the meal or the table prepared by the Lord and "the house of the Lord," which may be the temple as the place where the psalmist offered sacrifices and had a thanksgiving meal. The open language of the psalm (see chaps. 2 and 4) does not allow one to prove conclusively such a setting

4. For Katharine Sakenfeld's study of *ḥesed* in the Hebrew Bible, see *Faithfulness in Action: Loyalty in Biblical Perspective* (Philadelphia: Fortress Press, 1985).

in life for this psalm. Its possibility, however, serves to heighten or make vividly concrete the point of the psalm, that God is the secure protector and provider of security. From this point of view the psalm reflects not merely a general situation of trust in God. The psalmist has experienced real and fearful distress at some point in his or her life, a crisis that threatened to overwhelm and destroy. The marvelous confidence and trust arises out of the reality of God's delivering help.

Such an understanding of the psalm is reinforced by its literary context, specifically its sequential relationship to Psalm 22. To read it after hearing the anguished cry of distress and God's answering word of deliverance in Psalm 22 is to realize why and how such deep trust in God's protecting care is possible. It is one such as the lamenter of Psalm 22, transformed by God's saving grace into a loud and joyous witness to the goodness and steadfast love of God, who sings the twenty-third Psalm. If one wishes to know whence comes such abiding confidence and conviction of God's care, read Psalm 22 as a preface to Psalm 23. In this case the order of the psalms is a helpful clue to understanding and appropriating their meaning.

Some have suggested that Psalm 22 may have been originally the lament and praise of a king and Psalm 23 "the utterance of a royal head and representative of the community."[5] Whether or not that is the case, one of the most powerful contemporary interpretations of Psalm 23 is that of Leonard Bernstein in his composition "Chichester Psalms," where it is juxtaposed with the royal Psalm 2 (see my earlier exposition of Psalm 2). The sense of peace, assurance, and tranquillity arising out of the imagery of the shepherd and his flock is re-created musically as chorus and countertenor sing the twenty-third Psalm in lyric tones. Suddenly in the midst of this beautiful quiet melody there erupt, from Psalm 2, the harsh, rapid, and loud sounds of the kings raging and plotting together against the Lord's anointed. This tumult takes over and would seem to be in control, but slowly above the din one begins to hear the voice of the countertenor singing the dominant line (musically and exegetically) of Psalm 23: *'ădōnay rō'î; lō' 'eḥsār*, "The Lord is my shepherd; I shall not want." Gradually the voices of the powerful rulers sputter out and only the melody of trust is left.

Psalm 23 is, therefore, a psalm of deep confidence, a confession of faith or trust in God that may have arisen out of a concrete experience of danger that the psalmist underwent. But it is not simply an expression

---

5. J. H. Eaton, *Kingship and the Psalms* (London: SCM Press, 1967), 76.

of thanksgiving for a moment of deliverance. The psalmist extrapolates from that experience and the whole of life a confession that God will always exercise personal care, giving both provision for life and protecting support. The psalmist in this case does not simply pray for this but claims the certainty of enjoying it. The psalm belongs to the faith vocabulary of the Old Testament. It has been properly recognized as a primal declaration of both (a) the basic trust of the one who knows he or she belongs to God, and (b) the nature of God's care for those who belong to the Lord. The psalm is intimate and personal. The use of the first-person singular is an indication of this and an important vehicle for carrying it over into the ongoing community, as is also its literary setting in the hymnbook of Israel and the church. Those things have properly enabled the psalm's appropriation through the ages by individual members of the ongoing community of faith.

The unfailing use of this psalm in Christian funerals is a clue to what present context may be its best locus. It may properly belong to the end of life when one can look back on the experience of a lifetime, out of which comes confidence about the future and God's ongoing care. It is not inappropriate in the face of death—the valley of deepest shadow, the last enemy, the darkest threat. In the context of Christian faith, Jesus Christ as the Good Shepherd is the seal upon the confidence of the one who trusts (John 10:11–12). He is the one we know as Shepherd, both in his promised care of the flock and in his laying down his life for them. He is the host at the table, which represents the victory over all enemies, over death. The shepherd imagery continues on in Christ; so also the banquet imagery in the Eucharist and in the anticipation of the eschatological messianic banquet at the end of days: "Lo, I am with you always, even unto the end of the age."

"God has taken his place in the divine council;
in the midst of the gods he holds judgment."

PSALM 82

In this psalm we enter a different world of thought from what one seems to encounter in most of the other psalms, though it has affinities with a number of other Old Testament texts. It is not a psalm that has been significant in the history of piety or worship. For Psalm 82 is one of the most overtly mythological texts in Scripture, which in its form and content seems to touch base hardly at all with anything familiar to most persons in the community of faith. There is no "I" or "we" uncovering the anguish of a troubled heart or lifting exultant praise to the glory of God. The psalm is not even set in the world we know. It has its setting in the divine council or the heavenly assembly,[1] a mythological motif common to the religious world of the ancient Near East, in which the gods gather together as a political or judicial assembly or on occasion as a military entourage, often, if not usually, under the direction or leadership of one of the high gods. In Psalm 82 one enters that world, encountering at the very beginning the heavenly assembly with the gods seated all about. The psalm looks as if it could have come straight out of Canaanite mythology. It has very little, if any point of contact with the contemporary reader of the psalms for whom the whole notion of a heavenly assembly or a council of the gods is only a mythopoeic way of speaking, an image that seems out of place in the modern world, even in the modern theological world where the most obvious demythologization of the notion of God has eliminated at the first stage the idea of God on a heavenly throne surrounded by other divine beings.

---

1. On this motif see E. T. Mullen, Jr., *The Assembly of the Gods: The Divine Council in Canaanite and Early Hebrew Literature* (Chico, Calif.: Scholars Press, 1980).

The fact, however, that we are dealing here with imagery and mythological form that would probably not be a vehicle for the expression of
faith in contemporary theology does not mean that we cannot search for
the intention of the ancient imagery of the Near East. For in such extended metaphors the people of Israel expressed some rather basic convictions about the God who had brought them into being and claimed
their life. They used the thought forms, the language, the images that
were given to them out of their environment, but they used them and
transformed them in the service of a particular view of the intention and
purpose of God in the human community, a view that in some way
reaches its strongest expression in this psalm as it speaks about two of
the foundation stones of the faith of Israel and indeed the whole Judeo-
Christian tradition: monotheism and the place of justice in the human
arena.

Psalm 82 is, in effect, a brief dramatic scene in the affairs of the assembly of the gods. In this scene Elohim, God, stands up (v. 1) in the midst
of the gods (*elohim*), and turning the divine council into a judicial court,
proceeds to act as a judge *against the other gods*. Elohim first utters a series of indictments against the gods that are composed both of accusations about misconduct (v. 2) and commands that define and call for
proper divine conduct (vv. 3–4). The powerlessness or incompetence of
these gods to carry out their responsibility for ensuring justice is described in v. 5 in language reminiscent of the description in Isaiah 40—
55 of the nothingness of the idols that have no capacity to see or know or
discern anything, and the earthshaking effect of this failure or incompetence is disclosed. The final act of judgment by Elohim is a sentence
pronounced against all the other gods, which is to the effect that those
who are gods shall die like mortals (v. 6), those who are eternally exalted
in their divine status shall now be brought low, as is eventually the
case with every human ruler (v. 7). At the conclusion to the psalm, the
psalmist calls for Elohim, God, to rise up and judge the earth, claiming
as an inheritance or permanent possession all the nations whose gods
are now eliminated from the scene.

What does all this talk about the gods and the council of the gods have
to do with monotheism? It seems strangely incongruous as an expression of faith of a people who claimed the Lord of Israel as God of the universe and worthy of the worship of all peoples. What in effect is happening, however, is that the issue of whether the universe is ruled by
one or many, whether the ground of being is divided or whole, whether
the object of ultimate human loyalty and devotion is single or divided,

whether the human community is seen to be under the claim of one Lord or several, is being addressed head-on in these verses. With the image of the divine council, which is pervasive in the Old Testament and can hardly be expunged from that literature without significant damage and loss, Israel knew itself to be speaking about the divine governance of the world. With this psalm it makes for its time a radical statement that suggests a permanent shift in the way that issue is to be understood by the human community, a shift that has had enduring effect even though the polytheistic option still holds many adherents. Not even the central Christian revelation, the incarnation of God in Jesus Christ, altered that claim. Indeed Christian theology reasons and Christian faith confesses that Jesus of Nazareth merits the title of Lord and the absolute devotion of *all* human beings precisely because in this one is revealed the *one* God of all.[2]

Some have seen Psalm 82 as a stage in the development toward monotheism. In some ways that is what I am suggesting, but one must be hesitant about arguing any chronological step or assuming that after this psalm is created it is no longer possible to talk about the gods of the divine world. That is simply not the case. Israel lived in a world peopled with gods, and the revelatory mode of God always works its way in continuity with and out of the human modes of thinking and understanding even at the point of sharp discontinuity and disjunction.[3] What happens here is that the divine world is rendered impotent and totally powerless before the God of Israel. We have here no other named deities. We have no battle among the gods (though remnants of that are present elsewhere in the Old Testament). The gods are nameless, colorless, silent. Even the reference to them uses the same term—*elohim*—that is used for the God who totally overwhelms all other claims to deity, suggesting a kind of integration into Elohim of all *elohim* reality or claims to reality. Whatever this psalm refers to by way of "gods" has no autonomy or independence apart from Yahweh-Elohim, the Lord, the God of Israel.

In the midst of this assembly of the gods, the Lord rises and in explicit, and to my knowledge unprecedented, fashion condemns all the other deities to death. The condemning of one god to death by another god or group of gods, or mortal combat between individual gods or

2. For some reflections on the centrality of the monotheistic claim in the Old Testament and its implications for human existence see my essay, "The Most Important Words: The Yoke of the Kingdom," *The Iliff Review* 41 (1984): 17–30.

3. See the elaboration of this point in my article "God and the Gods: History of Religion as an Approach and Context for Bible and Theology," *Affirmation* 1/5 (1973): 37–62.

groups of gods, is not uncommon in religious mythologies. But the claim that *one* deity renders *all other* deities *mortal* is another matter. While I assume it is not impossible that one might discover this motif sometime in the context of Near Eastern myth, it seems highly unlikely. Whether or not there are any analogies, the force of the mythopoeic act described in this psalm should not be missed. The whole divine world is rendered or asserted to be impotent. The psalm is the story of the death of the gods. The immortals are condemned to the fate of mortality and merit comparison with human beings and not God. In this sense the gods are clearly and permanently negated. Only the Lord of Israel can claim the just rule (which is the meaning of "judge the earth" in v. 8) of all the earth. Only God, Elohim, has any power in the divine realm. There is, therefore, a sense in which one can say that while the reader of this psalm enters the world of the gods at the beginning of the psalm, he or she has left it forever at the end of the psalm. The imagery of the divine council remains a part of the powerful language by which the Old Testament dramatically expresses the Lord's rule and governance, but the life of the gods is at an end. Human worship has only one direction; human life has only one aim. Not only is divided loyalty in an ultimate sense no longer a part of the structure of the universe. It is, in Israel's faith, which we inherit, now seen to be a problem to be overcome. To the extent that that happens, human life is made whole, no longer torn apart.

Of equal importance to the final outcome of the psalm is the particular impetus that brings about the negation of the divine world. The gods are condemned to death for their failure to carry out justice in the human realm, a justice that is particularly characterized by protecting and maintaining the right of the weak and powerless members of the community as represented especially in the widow, the orphan, the poor, the oppressed—indeed those persons who on their own do not have the capacity to claim their own place and are vulnerable to those with wealth and power, who can become the wicked as they oppress and overwhelm the weak for their own enhancement. The courts and the marketplace are first in view in God's indictment of what is wrong and call for what is "right" (v. 3b), but all the structures of society small or large are in view when the issue of divine governance of the human realm is at stake.

How much does justice in human society matter? Israel never gave a clearer or more radical answer to that question, even in the strongest words of Amos and Jeremiah, Isaiah and Micah, than in this psalm. Justice is the cornerstone of the universe. The notion that justice matters was not a discovery of Israel's religion. But the intensity and centrality of righteousness and justice are a particular touchstone of that tradition, which has never been diminished. Justice in the *human* realm was a concern of all Near Eastern religions, but in Psalm 82 the *cosmic* realm also depends upon justice in the social order. Indeed the very foundations of cosmic order are shaken in the presence of injustice. The cosmos, the universe, the divine world, depends upon the maintenance of justice in the human community — not only in Israel's midst but in *all* communities. When justice is not maintained, then the very foundations of the earth are shaken, the world threatens to fall apart into chaos once more. That is how much justice matters. It is not just one of the virtues. It is not even a high ethical demand. Justice is the issue on which the very claims of deity are settled. Justice, just rule, is that central activity by which God is God. Without it the very universe cannot survive.

PSALM 90

The primary locus in which the Christian community regularly hears this psalm is the funeral or memorial service. Along with Psalm 23 it is probably read more often than any other passage from the Old Testament, though vv. 7–9 and 11–12 are not infrequently omitted, as indeed they are in the psalm as it is printed in the Book of Common Worship that has been used in Presbyterian churches in this country for decades. One understands this omission immediately. These Old Testament words about human life being overwhelmed by the wrath of God hardly seem to be the most obvious words of comfort.

Still the psalm—in whole or in part—has a large capacity to bring the strong comfort of God to persons on sickbeds and in times of dying and death. The reasons for that are probably many. As one reads and studies the psalm, however, the heart of the matter seems to be that Psalm 90 is helpful in moments of preparation for death, or of grief at the time of death, because of the way it speaks about all the time before death and helps us think about that, with respect to one who has died and with respect to our own time. The content of vv. 1–2, the six references each to "days" and "years," as well as the several references to "morning" and "evening," are the chief clues to the character of the psalm as a reflection and prayer about time and more particularly *our* days (vv. 9, 12, 14) and *our* years (vv. 9, 10: "the days of our years"). The psalm addresses in various ways the question, In the sure knowledge of our death, what gives meaning to our time now and how should we understand our time from the perspective of that moment when our life is at an end? (The

125

first-person plural is used throughout this exposition because the tone and language of the psalm elicit it.)

In seeing how the psalm speaks to that question, it is necessary to pay attention to the movement and logic of the psalm. It begins with an introductory word about God (vv. 1–2) and then moves to an extended statement about human mortality in the light of God's eternity and God's wrath (vv. 3–10). This section is similar in ways to the complaint dimension of the lament psalms, but it has a reflective tone, which has something to do with the tendency to appropriate this psalm in reflecting upon death. Verses 11–12 form a transition from the preceding (in v. 11) and into the series of petitions (v. 12) that represent a view of what human beings can expect and ask of God for the limited time of human life.

One of the things this movement does is to suggest that finding meaning in our life *now* in the face of death *then* depends upon placing the starting point of our understanding outside ourselves (vv. 1–2). That is a rather difficult thing to do when dealing with the expectation of our death, but according to the psalm it is the proper thing to do. For the beginning of the psalm is a clue to where one can and should begin the search for meaning in the time we are given. It opens with a double word about God that is awesome in its claim—awesome both in the breadth of the claim and in the way it instills in us both encouragement and awe, which are not necessarily the same thing and may even be at odds with each other. Using creation imagery drawn from the experience of a woman giving birth, the psalm declares the transcendence and eternity of God:

> Before the mountains were born,
>   or you had brought forth in labor
>   the earth and the world,
>   from everlasting to everlasting you are God.
>   (v. 2; my trans.)

> For a thousand years in your sight
>   are but as yesterday when it is past.
>   or as a watch in the night.
>   (v. 4; my trans.)

Before ever we turn to think about *our* time, or *as* we think about our time, we are reminded of a prior reality—the time of God. That, of course, is not particularly a comforting word. Indeed, as the psalm says, it tends to make us all too aware of how quickly we pass away. But this

word is a proper perspective, a reminder of the "Godness" of God before we turn to think about our humanity. And that is the context in
which meaning in human life in some ultimate sense may be possible.
For alongside, and even prior to (in the structural movement of the
psalm), this rather overwhelming assertion about God that seems to re-
duce our humanity, our time, to nothingness, is the declaration that this
God who brought forth the universe, who was there before it came to be
and will be there after it is gone, *that* God is *our refuge*. The *first* word, the
foundation word, is the claim (v. 1):

> Lord, thou hast been our dwelling place
>   in all generations.

There is no moment in all of our time that we have not been in God's
hands. God is the one in whom we live and move and have our being
and in whom we can ask the question about our life in the face of death.

Now alongside—and indeed growing out of this conviction about
God as the context of our life—there is another important dimension to
the way in which the psalm speaks of our time. That is its utter *realism*
about human life under God. It reminds us in inescapable fashion that
our life is clearly limited and that we must perceive it and deal with it as
such. One of the great human self-deceptions is to think of our time as
unlimited when in fact, as this psalm reminds us, our time is short; for
all of us death comes, and it is no illusion.

But this realism about the limitation of life that rings throughout the
ninetieth Psalm also involves the realization that our finitude and mortality are not accidents but arise out of the will and purpose of God, who
both limits our days and judges them for their sin. In this matter we
have to deal with God. That is what the psalm means in its words about
the anger of God. It does not mean that we have to deal with a capri-
cious, arbitrary God who may not like us or who turns our life into absurdity by cutting short our days. It does mean that the one who is the
ground of our being has created us for lives that manifest love and righteousness, that continue the good purposes for which God has brought
this universe into being; and that the universal failure so to live places
our lives under the limitation and judgment of death.

Various biblical stories illustrate this reality, but the primary (and primal) one is the story of the man and woman in the Garden of Eden,
driven from it to lives of toil and the limitation of death because they do
not obey the command of God and live out the good purpose of God.

Karl Barth in his discussion of "ending time" has given theological expression to the poetic discernment of the psalmist:

> Death as it actually encounters us men [!] is the sign of God's judgment on us . . . the finitude of human life stands in fact in the shadow of its guilt. . . . In its perhaps concealed but very real basis our fear of death is the well-grounded fear that we must have of God. But this is to say that at the point where we shall be at our end, it is not merely death but God Himself who awaits us. . . . But the God who awaits us in death and as the Lord of death is the gracious God. . . . It is really true that we need not fear death, but God. But we cannot fear God without finding in him the radical comfort which we cannot have in any other. But this simply means that it is God who is our Helper and Deliverer in the midst of death.[1]

More specifically in relation to this psalm, Walter Harrelson has seen the relationship between God's wrath and the possibility of human life's having purpose and significance:

> God does not leave human beings alone but comes into their lives. God insists that human life, fleeting and apparently pointless though it be, be a responsible life. . . .

Thus it is, as Harrelson notes, that it is the wrath of God that finally constitutes hope:

> [T]he wrath of God is the clearest sign to a faithful and struggling community that there is purpose in life. . . . God's wrath is a constant and relentless pressure felt by the faithful in their lives, a presence that warns and admonishes and requires the securing of wisdom that it may be detected the better.[2]

This psalm, however, does not end in reflection on our mortality and God's involvement in it. It culminates in a series of prayers (vv. 12–17) that implicitly summon readers and hearers of the psalm to pray and anticipate that God will help human beings find meaning for life in the certainty of death, and it suggests in the course of those prayers some of the ways in which the meaning of time, of our days and years, is to be found.

1. "Teach us to number our days that we may get a heart of wisdom" (v. 12). This is a prayer to God to help us perceive life as not only brief but *allotted* time. Learning to number our days is not simply to become

---

1. Karl Barth, *Church Dogmatics* III/2 (Edinburgh: T. & T. Clark, 1960), 596, 607–10.
2. Walter Harrelson, "A Meditation on the Wrath of God: Psalm 90," in *Scripture in History and Theology*, ed. A. L. Merrill and T. W. Overholt (Pittsburgh: Pickwick Press, 1977), 190.

aware that at some point they will end, but even more that God has *given* us time—a point that even such an agnostic as Ecclesiastes affirms again and again—that is fraught with opportunity and possibility. The psalmist in effect prays to God that we do not fail to see our time. For when we do see that our time is allotted time, then the response is not resignation, which, as Barth has properly noted, is incompatible with the fact that life is created by God,[3] but gratitude and joy that this time has been given to us. Precisely because it is created *by* God and *for* God, it has—again to use Barth's language—"an unfathomable and inexhaustible reality."

2. "Satisfy us in the morning with your steadfast love that we may rejoice all our days" (v. 14). Allotted time, therefore, has a quality to it and is filled not simply with time and routine but with the gift of God. It is hardly an accident that one of the passages most closely analogous to Psalm 90's depiction of human life as being like grass that is renewed and flourishes but then fades and withers (vv. 5–6) is Ps. 103:15–17, which depicts human existence exactly the same way but then contrasts that with the steadfast love of God, which is as enduring as God is. It is that sense of the constancy and availability of God's love (*ḥesed*) that the psalmist draws upon here, knowing that nothing is more capable of filling or satisfying our days than the experience of the mercy and the graciousness of God in all those moments when we need it. The temporal reference "in the morning" is clearly tied to the earlier comparison of human life to grass flourishing "in the morning" (two times in vv. 5–6). Here the prayer maintains the realism of the first part of the psalm. The petition "satisfy us in the morning" may echo the frequent indications elsewhere that God's help is sought or comes "in the morning" after the dark night of terror and/or vigil, but in this psalm it is clear that those who know that evening comes for every life, pray in anticipation that the morning of life may flourish like rich green grass when the steadfast love of God is present. That is what "satisfies," gives meaning and value to life. And that gracious love is, therefore, sufficient.

3. "Make us glad as many days as you have afflicted us, and as many years as we have seen evil" (v. 15). This is a modest prayer. One might even call it ironic if it were not so consistent with the rest of the psalm. It reflects again the realistic piety of Israel that does not hide the fact that much of life is pain and toil. So it instructs us to hope and pray that in God's providence God may see not that pain is eliminated from our time

3. Barth, *Church Dogmatics* III/2:555.

but that we are provided with as much happiness as pain. The psalmist does not measure the quality of life by the question, Is everything perfect? but expects that God will see that the joy matches the burden. If that seems to smack a little of hedonism, then perhaps the psalm does suggest to us that a calculus of pain and pleasure is not altogether inappropriate for human life, but as a prayer to the heart of God more than a philosophy of life. That prayer does assume that in this measure of pain and happiness individual existence can find some of its value and possibility.

4. "Let your work be manifest to your servants and your glorious power to their children" (v. 16). The prayer is simply that we may be open to and aware of what God is doing in the world. It is highly doubtful that we can find some ultimate meaning simply in our own lives and experience. Within the reality and limitations of existence that are described so clearly in this psalm, any search for value in an *ultimate* sense in our three score years and ten is likely to seem an absurdity; but that may happen as we are taken outside ourselves to discern the work of God, to learn "what it's all about" and that our individual lives and our communal life have their place in that divine purpose (cf. Psalm 8).

5. That obviously does not mean, however, that our own life and work are meaningless in the face of the fact that we are soon gone. On the contrary, Psalm 90 concludes with the prayer: "Let the favor of the Lord our God be upon us, and establish the work of our hands upon us; indeed establish it upon us" (v. 17). The final prayer is that we may be confirmed in our *own* work and calling, that in some way God will make secure what we do, will give our work a place. This is not a prayer for fame and greatness, nor a prayer that we may see the fulfillment, the consequence, the outcome of our work, but that it may be established, that is, that God may bring whatever work we do into being and give it enduring value. We may or may not see the shape and outcome of our work, but we may ask God to bring it to fruition and so place the work of our hands in God's hands.

Thus does Psalm 90 set before us our final time as a perspective from which to view all our time.

"Unless the Lord builds the house,
those who build it labor in vain."

PSALM 127

Filled with rich and powerful images, Psalm 127 is one of the most familiar of the Songs of Ascents (Psalms 120—134), functioning for the community of faith in a variety of ways from the happy celebration of the birth of a child as the gift of God (v. 3), to reassurance and comfort in the face of grief and death (v. 2), to the instruction and guidance of civic or political leaders (v. 1). It is no wonder—and singularly appropriate —that Benjamin Franklin set these words before Congress as it began to draft a constitution for the United States of America[1] or that John F. Kennedy in one of his addresses reminded the nation that without God's aid his labors were in vain and the nation could not be built or secured.

There is fairly widespread consensus that Psalm 127 is composed of two sayings of a wisdom character, one having to do with the vanity of building a house, protecting a city, and human toil without the Lord's power, the other affirming the blessing of God's gift of children. While some interpreters have regarded these two parts as originally separate and only artificially unified, the two sections are clearly held together in a unity that transcends the apparently different subject matter. At a surface level, they are bound together by their beginning with key words that have different meanings but the same sounds: *bānāh*, "build," and *bānîm*, "sons," "children." Even more important, the "house" that is built in v. 1 must be related to the sons or children that are the heritage of the Lord in vv. 3–5. That can be seen by looking closely at the Psalm

---

1. R. E. Prothero, *The Psalms in Human Life* (London: John Murray, 1904), 232.

and particularly at the various *contexts* in which the language of the different parts may be seen.

Ps. 127:1–2. The determinative phrases in v. 1 are "builds the house" and "watches over the city." The initial expression with the Lord as the subject of the verb can have several meanings in the light of use of the same phrase in other psalms and elsewhere. "Building" as a divine activity can refer to God's building the sanctuary (Ps. 78:69) or Jerusalem (Pss. 102:16 and 147:2) or David's throne (Ps. 89:4). There are some contexts that speak more specifically of the Lord's building a *house* (as is the case in Ps. 127:1). These regularly have to do with a family line or a dynasty, as in God's promise to build a sure or faithful house for the priest who is faithful (1 Sam. 2:35). The promise to David is that God will build a house for him (2 Sam. 7:27; cf. 1 Chron. 17:10).

The expression "build the house" in v. 1 also refers to human activity. As such it can refer to human procreation (Deut. 25:9; Ruth 4:11; cf. Gen. 16:2; 30:3) as well as to human toil to build a physical structure (e.g., Gen. 33:17; Deut. 8:12). More specifically the "house" can be and indeed is in key places a palace or temple. In 2 Sam. 7:13 (= 1 Chron. 17:12), the Lord's building a house for David, that is, a dynasty, is paired with David's son's building a house, that is a temple for the Lord's name. Solomon's building activities center in the temple-palace complex, which serves to provide a house for himself and the Lord. The kingship of Solomon under the rule of God is manifest in the building of a house (see below on the superscription).

The expression "build a house" is capable, therefore, of having varying meanings or connotations. In this context, it could refer to any or all of the following activities (divine and human): building Zion or the sanctuary; building the palace or temple; building the Davidic line or house; or building anyone's line or house. Physical structures, family households, and human communities all come under the possible purview of v. 1a.

Verse 1b then introduces the parallel theme and moves from the house to the city: "If the Lord does not keep watch over the city, the sentry stays awake in vain." Again the point is the vanity or fruitlessness of human efforts apart from the Lord's involvement and activity. This time that activity is the protection and security of a city, that is, of the human community. The verb "watch over," *šāmar*, describes a very basic function or activity of God.[2] Psalm 121 is centered entirely on the expres-

2. Paul Riemann, "Am I My Brother's Keeper," *Interpretation* 24 (1970): 482–91.

sion of confidence in the Lord's "keeping watch," but that theme runs throughout the psalms (25:20; 34:20; 86:2; 97:10; 116:6). It is one of the fundamental blessings in the Aaronic benediction (Num. 6:24). In most cases Israel or human beings are the objects of the Lord's keeping. Here it is a city. One may assume the line is not just an image or analogy but that a real city is meant. That is indicated both by the fact that we are dealing with one of the Songs of Ascents probably connected in some way to pilgrimage or procession at Jerusalem, and also by the parallel to "house." The reference to house and city in parallel lines suggests that we are dealing with real structures of some sort. At the primary level the city may be Jerusalem. But the word "city" here is richly ambiguous. It may be Jerusalem, or it may be any city, that is, the city of those who sing this song.

It becomes clear already, therefore, that the nature or identity of the house the Lord builds is very much determined by the context in which one places it. Verse 1b, which parallels v. 1a precisely, leads one to think of the house there as the Jerusalem temple. But vv. 3–5 as the larger context for interpreting the house that is built by the Lord suggest that may be a family line.

A third potentially useless or empty activity is described in v. 2. The ones whose efforts are in vain here are those who rise up early, delay resting, and eat the bread of painful toil, that is, those who work cease-lessly and arduously, hardly getting sufficient rest. The specific refer-ence of "rest" (v. 2a) is not certain. It could mean sitting down to rest or sitting down to eat (as, e.g., in Exod. 32:6). The context enables one to place those possible meanings together and understand the sitting as any sort of cessation of labors. The meaning of the word translated "sleep"— *šēnā'*—in the RSV is difficult to determine. It is quite doubtful that it means "sleep." More likely it means either "prosperity" or "honor."[3] The first part of the verse, therefore, refers to those who seek to attain wealth or high position by the drive of their own achievements, presumably without looking to God for help or placing their labors in God's hands. Such activity and efforts are ultimately empty. The Lord is the one who gives wealth and honor.

The interpreter should not miss the echoes of Gen. 3:17–19 in the first colon of v. 2b. It is precisely "eating bread in anxious toil" that is the judgment on the primeval man who disobeyed the Lord (Genesis 2—3). In the context of the Genesis primeval history, which is also seen in the background of the blessing-of-children theme that follows, Psalm 127

3. See the extended discussion of the various interpretations of this word by J. A. Emer-ton, "The Meaning of *šēnā'* in Psalm cxxvii 2," *Vetus Testamentum* 24 (1974): 15–31.

here places a negative judgment on the approach to life that centers in constant driving of oneself in laborious, anxious, hard work. It claims that such a way of going about the human enterprise of work is as useless, vain, empty, and without effect as seeking to build a house or secure a city without God's active involvement. In some respects that seems to be a counterword to Gen. 3:17–19, which suggests that eating the bread of anxious toil is the actual and appropriate destiny of human beings who have disobeyed God. Yet the psalm is probably more in continuity with the primeval history (Genesis 1—11) at this point, for in the Cain and Abel story we read that because of Cain's violence against his brother, Cain—who is the representative human figure in this story —will work the earth in vain (Gen. 4:12).

Now, the story in Genesis 1—11 does move to tell of God's gracious lifting of the curse. But there remains throughout the Old Testament a rather negative tone as one dimension of how it understands human work. The nature of that negative tone may best be seen here in Psalm 127, which does not condemn human work. Indeed it speaks about human labor (*'āmāl*) in v. 1, but it makes two points that have to be kept in mind. Even labor (*'āmāl*), proper human work to create the structures of life and provide for them, is useless without God's effective participation, grounding or undergirding that work. And second, hard or anxious toil (*'ăṣṣabîm*), defined here as a frantic, racing, ceaseless involvement in work, is useless, period, because God is the one who gives prosperity and honor. So along with the negative understanding of some kinds or ways of working, v. 2 sets a grace note. It may be understood in one of two ways and it is hard to be absolutely sure which is intended: either God gives the divine gift instead of that sort of anxious toil, or to those human beings who are caught in such anxious hard labor, God gives God's gift.

Ps. 127:3–5. The theme of these verses is clear and consistent—the joy and reward of having children, who provide blessing and security.[4] Three points are scored simply. One is the understanding that children are a divine gift. This is a notion that runs throughout the Old Testament and is in danger of being lost in the modern world when it is viewed in the abstract or as a general statement. The problems of over-

4. The psalm seems to have in view primarily sons and the father rather than children and parents in general. The contemporary community can and should interpret the psalm in a more inclusive way, recognizing the joy and reward for both mothers and fathers in having both sons and daughters; the original intention was probably more male-oriented.

population and unwanted children, even the painful moral dilemma of abortion, seem to press upon us the possibility that the gift and blessing has been turned into a curse. But these genuine and serious problems that arise out of the act of procreation, which like every human act is complex, morally ambiguous, and consequential even as one claims the mystery of God's involvement, should not be allowed to overshadow the even larger experiential reality that children are one of the richest manifestations of the blessing of God on human life and one of the clearest points where people sense the mystery and joy of God's gift. The psalm then goes on to elaborate the sense of reward in a functional way using the simile of arrows in a quiver to speak of children as the weapons of a warrior, that is, as security against adversity. The final line is somewhat enigmatic and unclear in the Hebrew but seems to speak of the success of the family when they contend with adversaries in the law court. The particularity of the Israelite situation, that is, with respect to the local court and family clan, or town conflicts, may not immediately touch the contemporary sense about the positive role that children, sons and daughters, play in the life of parents, but the underlying notion, to wit, that parents can find both joy and security in their children, may have its manifestation in many ways. It is the task of the interpreter to point to some of those ways concretely, whereby even with all the pain, anxiety, and distress that parents experience always with children, they nevertheless find the deepest joys in them also. Further, there are few parents who do not look for and indeed find their children as a source of security and protection in the face of adversity. There are exceptions to all this, of course, as indeed there certainly were in Israel's experience. Look at David, the one to whom the psalms are most often ascribed, and that will be clear. But the real exceptions should not overshadow or cause us to lose sight of the larger reality, experienced in similar and dissimilar ways, in the passing of time, to which this psalm points.

It should be noted, as we ask what the sentences of this psalm mean in varying contexts, that placing the picture one has from vv. 3–5 after vv. 1–2 leads to a hearing and understanding of the second part of the psalm in the light of the first. One is not likely to enjoy children as blessing unless the "house" that is built in and through them is built by and under the Lord. The *bānāh* (build)–*bānîm* (children) connection holds together the two parts in a single whole. But the admonition of the first part has moved to a positive assurance and declaration. The transition is in the final part of v. 2, which clearly belongs to the first part of the psalm but anticipates the second part by moving from speaking of the

Lord's involvement in the human activity (building and securing) in an admonitory fashion (v. 1) to a positive declaration of God's gift (v. 2b), which is the subject of the second part of the psalm. The children (v. 3), like honor or prosperity, are the Lord's gift which comes to those who place their lives and activities under the Lord's direction. In that sense the gift is a rich blessing to those who receive it.

There are two other contexts in which one may fruitfully place the words of the Psalm. One of these is the superscription, which in its first part, "A Song of Ascents," places the song in the context of a group of psalms (Psalms 120—134) that probably bear that title because they are seen as songs for pilgrimage up to the temple in Jerusalem. Most of them in one fashion or another refer to Jerusalem or Zion. The presence, therefore, of this rubric over Psalm 127 in effect allows and pushes the reader and interpreter to relate the house and city of v. 1 to the temple and Jerusalem specifically and beyond that to any human structures and communities where God will be at the center.

That point is carried even further in the rubric "Of Solomon" or "For Solomon." By its presence, the Psalm is set to speak to human builders, and its word is declared to be for Solomon and those who like him build a house for God, who build the human city to be the city of God. The superscription says to the reader and interpreter, If one wants to know specifically what v. 1 has in mind, look at Solomon, the master builder of houses (1 Kings 3:1–2; 7; 8:13; 9:1) and cities (2 Chron. 8:1–11). One cannot build a house for oneself or God without God's help. And one cannot protect it or ensure the security of the human community, even Jerusalem, without the Lord's watching over it.

Finally, one can hardly miss the fact that this psalm is followed by or paired with a psalm that also speaks of the blessing of children but as the reward for those who fear the Lord. The subject of Psalm 128 is the God-fearer. The body of the psalm describes the blessings that come to such a one: eating the fruit of the labor of your hands, blessing and good, and a fruitful wife and thus many children. The ties with Psalm 127 are many and thus press the reader to hear the two psalms in relation to each other. In addition to shared vocabulary such as "man," "blessed," "fruit," and "house," both psalms have to do with the blessing and reward of having children, use similes to describe that reward, and emphasize the number of them. In both cases a "lo" or "behold," *hinneh*, divides the psalm in two, and the last two lines of Psalm 128 combine the city and the house, in the sense of household, like the first two lines of Psalm 127.

Several implications grow out of these affinities: (1.) The combination of city and household in 128:5–6 suggests that the "city" of 127:1 is at some level of interpretation indeed Jerusalem, a particular city, and not just an image for safety. (2.) The unity of Psalm 127 is reinforced when it is viewed alongside Psalm 128, especially vv. 5–6. (3.) The house in Psalm 128 is so thoroughly the house of the family that the reader is pushed to read the similar Psalm 127 in a similar way. (4.) Psalm 128 contributes to a more holistic view of work when placed with Psalm 127. The blessing of Psalm 128 includes "[the food of] the labor [yĕgîaʿ] of your hands you shall surely eat." Here is a positive kind of labor which is blessed by God, the work of those who fear the Lord, who walk in the ways of the Lord. To labor apart from the Lord, in a frantic, ceaseless manner, is to experience toil, the vain labor.

The conclusion of Psalm 128 matches the beginning of Psalm 127 in keeping before the reader and listener both the *civic/social* sphere, where God's activity and guidance must be sought and whose good is blessing for the community, and the *family sphere*, which cannot be created apart from God but which can be a great blessing when established in the fear of God and under God's guidance. Indeed Psalm 127 encompasses the most fundamental of enterprises—the building and founding of human structures, the securing and protecting of community, the work and vocation of men and women, the building of home and family. The word of the psalm is that unless such enterprises become God's enterprises as those who build, watch, and labor seek the will and way of God and invoke God's presence and purpose in these activities, then there is an emptiness to them. They are without purpose or effect. When, however, the Lord is at the center of such endeavors, then those who so live may see the good of the city and their children's children.

"Out of the depths I cry to thee, O Lord!"

PSALM 130

The 130th Psalm belongs to that group of psalms known in the church's liturgy as the Penitential Psalms because they express so deeply and profoundly the thoughts, experiences, and feelings of the penitent sinners who cry out in anguish at the realization of their unrighteousness before the righteous God but who at the same time know their only hope is in the grace and mercy of the same righteous God. Luther called Psalm 130 one of the "Pauline Psalms" because he found in it the expression of that unmerited grace and forgiveness that are at the heart of the gospel and without which—even as the psalm so clearly declares—existence before God is not possible.

Countless others throughout the centuries have identified themselves with the psalmist who uttered these words. Augustine is said to have inscribed the words of the Penitential Psalms on the walls of his chamber during his last illness so that he could make their words his own. John Wesley heard the words of Psalm 130 sung as an anthem at St. Paul's Cathedral on the afternoon of the same day that brought him in the evening to the room at Aldersgate where, as he described it, he found his heart "strangely warmed." The prayer of Psalm 130 helped prepare him for the transforming experience of the grace of God that changed his life and ultimately the lives of hundreds and thousands of others.

All these have seen in the psalm a mirror on the human plight and a window to the divine forgiveness. "Out of the depths," its opening words, translated into Latin as *De profundis*, have become a title for the Psalm, not simply because they are the initial words but because they express a universal experience of despair and lostness. They evoke images and situations that lead the one who reads the psalm to cry out, "I have been there, too!" Thus it becomes the reader's or hearer's own prayer. The "depths" from which the psalmist cries are the deep, dark waters, an image that is capable of referring to various experiences: the nearness and threat of death, a spiritual abyss into which the mind and heart have fallen, a terrible overwhelming fear, the hostility and danger of enemies and foes. The language of the "depths" is as evocative on the contemporary scene as it was expressive to the ancient Israelite. Deep waters and murky depths continue to frighten us. Most of us pull back immediately when we come upon a deep pit for fear that we might find ourselves falling in it and lost forever. There is even a contemporary American slang expression, "That's the pits," meaning the worst sort of situation one can imagine. Closer to the force and meaning of the cry of the psalmist is the experience and anguish of being in the depths of despair or the depths of depression. The verses that follow indicate that in this case the fearful depths from which the cry goes up to God are not the threat of external or hostile forces but the mental, emotional, and spiritual dark night of the soul that finds itself plunged into sin and guilt, the broken relationship with God and neighbor, and is powerless to extricate itself from that predicament. The details of that sin and brokenness are not indicated at all. They need not be and indeed cannot be, for the iniquities of which the lamenter speaks embody all those multiple possibilities of acting against the will and purpose of God and against the freedom, integrity, and well-being of other persons.

The psalm speaks out of the paradoxical but very real and human experience of encounter with God that is the source of the despair in the depths and at the same time the only way out. Because there is a transcendent One whose righteous way has not been heeded and whose just order calls to account those who do not heed that way, the psalmist finds himself in an anguish of mind and heart that is nigh unto death. But that same righteous and transcendent God is the only hope or source of rescue from the depths, so that the response of the one who is mired in the depths is not a turning from the God who knows his or her iniquities, but a cry to God for deliverance. The human being who speaks in and through and with this psalm is a lamenter, a fact that signifies a dual reality: he or she is in the depths but also is one who prays. Those in the Bible who live their lives in relation to God are persons who move back and forth between petition and praise, between supplication for God's help and thanksgiving for the hope that comes. The experience of the depths does not take one out of that movement and that polarity but assumes that the first step is the anguished outcry to the One who is both problem and possibility. The way out of the depths begins in the possibility of prayer and the awareness that only the One who hears that prayer can draw us out of the depths. So the self that is caught in its iniquities cries out because of the need for forgiveness and because with *this* God forgiveness is possible.

To the extent that Psalm 130 portrays in some measure the human condition, it does so on the assumption that at every point one has to deal with God, that the human condition is not capable of transformation nor likely to be delivered except by God, that indeed the very experience of the depths arises out of our relation to God and the brokenness in the relation that our sins bring about. Release from the depths of despair and the abyss of sin and guilt comes not from the self-help of the one caught in that condition. It is to be found in the God whose nature is to forgive.

The corollary of the possibility of crying out from the depths is that there is One who hears and understands and responds. The responsiveness and understanding of God are what Gordon Kaufman in his *Systematic Theology* has called the perfections of the divine communing, the reality of God's presence with humanity. They point to the deeply personal character of the relationship, which manifests itself especially in the fact that God is subject to being moved, responsive, affected by the human cries out of the depths. As in all the laments of the Psalter, the desolate one over and over cries for the ear of God to be attuned to his or her plight, to hear the cry for help. Such cries are possible because of the knowledge that God understands and is responsive to the human situation, that God's promise to the one in trouble always remains: "If that one cries to me, I will hear, for I am compassionate" (Exod. 22:27). Amos 7:1–3, which bears a marked similarity to Psalm 130, beautifully expresses the thought that God is moved to compassion by the plight of people, even when their plight is the result of disobedience, rebellion, and estrangement (with the resultant overwhelming guilt). There, too, one who sees the pending, terrible fate of Israel prays against the righteousness and judgment of God:

> O Lord God, forgive, I beseech thee!
> How can Jacob stand?
> He is so small!

In both cases there is a tremendous sense of the impossibility of existing unforgiven before the righteousness of God. The absolute justice of God means clearly that, were the Lord to mark our sins, God would be justified in the sentence given and no one could endure before it. Psalm 130 recognizes in the cry to God from the depths a need for forgiveness. It is a need that has both an objective and a subjective character, external and internal dimensions. The external need lies in the fate of the guilty before the righteous judge, a fate seen by both Amos and the psalmist. The internal, subjective need is just as great. It is the sense of the depths, despair, isolation, and estrangement that can be overcome only by the initiative of God, not to mark or keep iniquities but to wipe them away, blot them out, in short to forgive.

That is, indeed, what happens because of the very nature of the God who confronts us and hears the prayer of the depths. Another attribute of the divine presence is, as Kaufman affirms, the forgiveness of God, which is the possibility of overcoming the guilt that casts us into the depths:

> When one has violated the confidence of another or betrayed him, his guilt clings like the bloody spots on Lady Macbeth's hands. No rationalization can destroy it, nor can the intervention or consolation of friends. A barrier is set up which cannot be overcome—except by the offended one's forgiveness. Only that personal act by the other self can overcome the estrangement and restore the positive relation. Forgiveness of another presupposes on the one hand, full recognition of the seriousness of the offense—while, on the other hand, the forgiving one "gives" up what he might rightly demand in view of the offense, freely offering to be reconciled.[1]

Prophet and psalmist alike perceive that the divine justice is governed, controlled, and dominated by grace—the prophet as he discerns God's turning away the judgment of Israel, the psalmist in his recognition that the nature of God is not to mark and keep iniquities but to forgive. While one may list ad infinitum the various attributes or characteristics of God, a summation of such a list would not discern what is the ground of the psalmist's trust: that the character of God is neither bent against us, nor neutral in God's justice and righteousness, but is bent toward us in grace and mercy. That is supremely the good news of the whole of Scripture, celebrated in the Christian church especially at Christmas and Easter, but apprehended constantly by individuals in their experience of being lifted out of the depths, of being dealt with graciously. The psalm expresses this way of God with individuals and with God's people three

1. Gordon D. Kaufman, *Systematic Theology: A Historicist Perspective* (New York: Charles Scribner's Sons, 1969), 241.

times with the same sort of expression, one that is both unusual and suggestive in its use of a preposition that signifies accompaniment:

with you there is forgiveness (v. 4)

with the Lord there is steadfast love (v. 7)

with him there is great redemption (v. 7)

Three fundamental characteristics—forgiveness, steadfast love or grace, and redemption—are set forth almost as intimate friends and companions of God. Wherever the Lord goes, they are there accompanying and going with God. To encounter this god is also to meet with grace and forgiveness and abundant redemption.

In the midst of these words of forgiveness one should not miss the clear indication that the ultimate aim of God's redemptive work even for the individual is the vindication of the divine purpose so that individuals and community are led to worship, serve, and fear the Lord (v. 4). This is a theme that runs throughout the Psalter and indeed the whole Bible. We hear it in Psalm 103:

> The steadfast love of the lord is
> from everlasting to everlasting
> upon those who fear him.
>   (v. 17)

And we hear it in Psalm 23:

> He leads me in paths of righteousness
> for his name's sake.
>   (v. 3)

In the New Testament also, the redemptive and forgiving work of God in Christ is understood as ultimately a testimony that calls others to acknowledge and worship that One who forgives. So the author of 1 John writes, ". . . your sins are forgiven for his sake" (2:12). And the Christ hymn of Philippians 2 ends with the declaration that the humiliation of Christ Jesus had its final outcome in God's exaltation of him "that at the name of Jesus every knee should bow, in heaven and on earth and under the earth, and every tongue confess that Jesus Christ is Lord, to the glory of God the Father" (vv. 10–11). The note that sounds in these various texts is a fundamental reminder of the theocentric character of human existence, even at the point when the self is most turned in upon and preoccupied with the self. The forgiveness of God that delivers from the depths of despair, guilt, and anxiety is not an end in itself but makes possible that glorification of God that is the primary end of all human life.

The one who grasps all this is on the way out of the depths via the medium of hope and anticipation (vv. 5–8). There is some uncertainty as to whether the verbs in v. 5 should be translated as present tense (e.g., "I wait"), signifying an already accomplished hope of forgiveness. The difference is largely academic. For even a present hoping has in mind clearly the eager and confident expectation of God's deliverance or God's word of forgiveness that is capable of totally transforming the being of the one in the depths. That transformation is beautifully expressed in Isa. 40:31:

> They who wait for the Lord shall renew their strength,
>   they shall mount up with wings like eagles,
> they shall run and not be weary,
>   they shall walk and not faint.

The one who looks forward to and confidently hopes in God's forgiving grace can experience such renewal. It is like changing into a whole new set of clothes. Even more appropriately, that hope, which waits with more tense anticipation than sentries in the late watch of the night waiting for dawn, furnishes the wings to lift one out of the depths. The image of the watchman is a powerful one and serves a double function. The psalms speak frequently of God's help in the morning, perhaps having in mind a response from God after all-night vigils and sacrifice in the sanctuary (cf. Pss. 3:5; 4:8; 5:3). But even more the image conveys a sense of one who is in the darkness, at any point subject to threats and danger, knowing that the dawn with its relief will come, but not yet out of the dark. The psalmist's expectancy of God's word and God's help is all that but even more so.

A final note is sounded in this psalm and it is heard over and over again in the Psalter. My experience with God is not exhausted by nor does it end with my personal deliverance and forgiveness. That forgiveness happens not only to bring about the worship of God (v. 4b), but the experience of the self is a witness to larger communities that points them to God's way of forgiveness and deliverance and calls forth from them a similar worship and praise (cf. 22:22–31; 69:30–36). What God does for the individual is reflected in the Lord's dealings with the community. Both individual and community are recipients of the grace of God, and the experience of one is always a reminder and call to the other to trust in the One who lifts us out of the depths.

"O Lord, thou hast searched me and known me!"

PSALM 139

In all of the psalms one senses how deep theological convictions are developed out of personal experience reflected on from the perspective of faith. Nowhere is that more evident than in this psalm, which, not surprisingly, is one of the best known to those who nurture their devotion to God on the psalms, while also being frequently cited by systematic theologians as they formulate a doctrine of God. One would not, of course, expect a single psalm to lay out a full constructive statement about God—and certainly not this one, precisely because it is highly personal and dialogical, formulated as conversation with God rather than formal statement about God. From beginning to end it is "I" and "you." It may translate into the poetic expression of Francis Thompson's "The Hound of Heaven" as easily as or better than into a systematic theological expression. It is poetry, rampant with figures of speech. The psalm, therefore, is not composed of careful, critical language, but it does express some profound thoughts about God that gain their validity as much out of their experiential authenticity as out of their presence in Scripture.

Psalm 139, however, despite its popularity, is also disturbing at some points, and those need to be addressed. Most obvious is the hatred of one's enemies that is expressed so vehemently in vv. 19–22. That theme will be dealt with below. Somewhat less shocking but also understandably resisted by Christian sensibilities is the fact that this is one of several psalms that seem to function primarily as protestations to God of the psalmist's innocence. In this case the chief clues to this intention on the part of the one praying are at the beginning and the end. Here is a person who knows the experience of having been examined minutely and wholly uncovered by God (vv. 1–6) and offers himself or herself for that examination again (vv. 23–24). The claim of innocence is probably made in the face of false accusations that have been raised against the psalmist (if the "wicked way" of v. 24 is actually the way of idolatry, as may well be the case, then that is probably an indication of the nature of the accusation). Such an assumption of innocence before God is foreign to Christian prayer, which customarily makes confession of sin before going on to supplication or petition. The assumption of a sinful state is the common presupposition of our prayer. One does not have to argue with that point of view to hear another possibility in this psalm, that is, the legitimacy of seeking divine response to a situation of need when one does not have a *particular* burden of guilt. The psalmist in this case is probably not claiming perfection of character, but neither does he or she cry, "Mea culpa, mea culpa, mea culpa!" The one praying comes to God not as sinner seeking forgiveness but as one who has walked and still desires (v. 24b) to walk in the Lord's way, the way of righteousness, and now seeks vindication before the all-seeing eye of God.

This is not a naive innocence unaware of the judgment of God upon all human failure to live as God would have us. On the contrary, the supplicant of Psalm 139 knows the possibility of God's hand falling heavy upon a person as well as being supportive. The psalm betrays some ambivalent feeling about this all-knowing God that is surely appropriate. But it also offers us the possibility of standing before God as those who have sought to be obedient and who, not claiming a general innocence, seek God's vindication in whatever form it may take, as well as God's continual guidance on the way the Lord would have us to go. That one will not, however, assume such a stance before God too lightly and quickly is an inference one may safely draw from a closer look at some of the things the psalm tells us about God.

THE DIVINE ATTRIBUTES

One familiar theological topic that seems to open out of this psalm is the character of God, more traditionally known as the attributes or perfections of God. Virtually everyone who reads the words of Psalm 139 senses the fact that it touches on the traditional attributes omniscience and omnipresence. These characteristics of God are probably as fully articulated here as anywhere in Scripture, but in these verses they have a liveliness and bite that needs to inform our more abstract analysis.

Omniscience. Most of us tend to approach this attribute of God quite logically. To talk about God means to exalt every human attribute to its perfection (the *via eminentiae*). Therefore, God who knows must know everything. The logic is as follows: God is personal; God knows; God must know all, for God is God. In Psalm 139, however, the conclusion is not reached logically but experientially: God's all-knowingness is inferred from the psalmist's experience that God knows all about *me*. There is nothing in the experience, the heart or mind of the person under God, that is not known to God. From the perspective of this psalm the overwhelming sense that before God all of one's being is uncovered is what omniscience is all about.

We probably touch base here with the *conscience*, that inward voice that affects what we do and say even before we do or say it (v. 4) and is often identified with the voice of the parent or culture but by the psalmist is found to be the voice, the mind of God that knows him or her, the Lord coming at "me" whatever direction "I" turn, burrowing into my innermost thoughts and mind.

Furthermore, what is being articulated by the psalmist is that *God* is the one who knows him or her (the "you" of v. 2 is emphatic: "*You* know when I sit down and when I rise up"), indeed in a way that no one else does, not even the one praying (v. 6). In dealing with omniscience what is at stake is usually perceived as an attribute of totality, that is, God's knowing everything, when here it is the knowledge of ourselves that no one else, including our innermost selves, can know. Whatever there is in our minds and hearts, bury it as deep as we can, and God will still know it. Whether that conforms to typical notions of divine "knowing all" or not, such knowledge may be the only thing that really *matters* in the omniscience of God.

Omnipresence. As Psalm 139 speaks of this attribute, again it is not in terms of a general statement about the being of God, logically derived, but rather in relation to some quite specific dimensions. The presence of God here, as in the New Testament, is linked with the Spirit of God. Indeed the Spirit is identified with God's presence by the parallelism of v. 7. The Gospel of John makes a similar claim: "And I will pray the Father, and he will give you another Counselor to be with you forever" (John 14:16). Positively, this is the psalmist's sense of the companion presence of God *with* the one who prays in every moment, every place, every circumstance. Again we encounter not a conviction about God's being generally present everywhere, though one might infer that; rather it is the certainty that God is present *everywhere I am* that the psalmist declares.

The cutting edge of that kind of omnipresence is the fact that at root it is really the *inescapability of God* that one encounters, a decidedly ambiguous reality as the psalm makes clear. Whatever my experience or fate, I am not cut off from the presence of God. But it is also the case that whatever I do, wherever I go, I cannot get away from God. To the suffering one who cries out in the dark night of the soul (or body) feeling abandoned by God, as, for example, the lamenter of Psalm 22, this dimension of God's character is truly good news. But to those who because of word or deed would flee from God, there is a truly unsettling aspect to God's inescapable presence. Ask Jonah; ask Achan (Joshua 7) or Ananias and Sapphira (Acts 5). Wherever we turn, God meets us as protecting and judging presence. Alluding to this psalm, Karl Barth has said that for the one whom God has created "there is no corner in which he does not exist for God, in which he is not enclosed by the hand of God behind and before. There is no heaven or hell in which he is out of the reach of God's Spirit or away from His countenance. There is no change or destruction in which his being before God and co-existence with Him are brought to an end and he escapes that which they always mean for him."[1]

PREDESTINATION

The doctrine of predestination is hardly one that is firmly rooted in the Old Testament Scriptures, but in Ps. 139: 13–16 we find some important expression of what that doctrine seeks to express. It has always been a theological claim that works better as a personal conviction about one's own destiny's being set in the purpose of God than it does as an effort to work out logically the mystery of God's purpose for others. That is, the knowledge that lies behind the doctrine is more surely a personal knowledge than it is deductive knowledge. So it is with the psalmist here, who eloquently asserts the prior work of God in his or her being brought into being, both in the complicated and unfathomable formation of a human life and in the determination of the psalmist's future. The imagery in vv. 13 and 15 is that of the divine weaver intricately weaving a variegated cloth. The poet sees himself not as an accident but

---

1. Karl Barth, *Church Dogmatics*, IV/1 (Edinburgh: T. & T. Clark, 1956), 482.

as one known, brought into being, given an allotted time, seen and encompassed by the everlasting God. What one hears in this test is that God knew us before we were born—not objectively or remotely but involved with our being, shaping our complex individuality and directing it toward our future, which is also God's future for us ("your book," v. 16). It is not unlike the word of the Lord to Jeremiah at the time of his call:

> Before I formed you in the womb I knew you,
>   and before you were born I consecrated you.
>   (Jer. 1:5)

Samuel Terrien in commenting on this psalm has defined predestination, especially as we see it here, as "the expression of a certainty, neither modest nor arrogant, of having been brought into existence for a mission which fits into God's grand design."[2] We do not encounter here a notion of having been elected or destined to a particular salvation but a sense of having been created in and out of the purposes of God, a certainty of having been called, even before our very being—there in the mind and knowledge and plan of God.

THE BEGINNING AND END OF
HUMAN EXISTENCE

As Psalm 139 concludes its hymnic reflection on God's involvement in our individual existence, we find this exclamation:

> How precious to me are your thoughts, O God!
>   How vast is the sum of them!
> If I would count them, they are more than
>   the sand.
> Were I to come to the end, I would still
>   be with you.
>   (vv. 17–18; my trans.;
>   see RSV footnote on 18b)

Here is both a tremendous word of assurance and a strong theological affirmation. There are two possibilities for what the last line means in its context, and they lead in the same direction. In light of the preceding colon, which makes the point that God's thoughts are innumerable, the psalmist may be declaring in effect, Were I to come to the end of God's

2. Samuel Terrien, *The Psalms and Their Meaning for Today* (New York: Bobbs-Merrill, 1952), 249.

thoughts, I would still be with God, led and held (v. 10) by God. That is, whatever limits I can think of, even to the thoughts of God, my being with God outruns them. Measuring the thoughts of God is beyond all comprehension, but even beyond that incomprehensibility the psalmist is sure that he or she is still somehow kept by God.

Or the psalm may be declaring, Even at *my* end I am still with you. Here is faith affirming that in our death we are caught up in the memory of God, remembered by God, held forever in the hand and mind and heart of God. That is probably the significance of the sentence "How *precious* to me are your thoughts, O God." They are precious in the eyes of the psalmist because he or she is always "in mind" with God. Those who pray with the speaker of this prayer know that God has known them before they even came into being. In like manner they claim in trust that God knows them after they go out of being, after they come to the end. Indeed they are compelled to that by the powerful sense that God has known them at all times. Most of us do not have any basic anxiety about our prebirth nonbeing but we tend to have that about our postdeath nonbeing. The psalmist, however, calls us to look at both states the same way. The end is no less clear in its basic character than the beginning. Whatever end we can conceive of finds us still with God.

If Psalm 139 is poetry become theology to make this point about God's eternal preservation, the following quotation from Karl Barth presses it home in the form of theology become poetry:

> The eternal preservation of the creature means positively—and this is the final point—that it can continue eternally before Him. God is the One who was, and is, and is to come. With Him the past is future, and both past and future are present. There was nothing that He could not perceive and know of all that began to be, and was, and was preserved by Him. Nothing could escape Him, or perish. Everything was open and present to Him: everything in its own time and within its own limits; but everything open and present to Him. Similarly, everything that is, as well as everything that was, is open and present to Him, within its own limits. And everything that will be, as well as everything that was and is, will be open and present to Him, within its own limits. And one day—to speak in temporal terms—when the totality of everything that was and is and will be will only have been, then in the totality of its temporal duration it will still be open and present to him, and therefore preserved: eternally preserved; revealed in all its greatness and littleness; judged according to its rightness or wrongness, its value or lack of value; but revealed in its participation in the love which He Himself has directed towards it. Therefore nothing will escape Him: no aspect of the great game of creation; no moment of human life; no thinking thought; no word spoken; no secret or insignificant enterprise or deed or

omission with all its interaction and effects; no suffering or joy; no sincerity or lie; no secret event in heaven or too well-known event on earth; no ray of sunlight; no note which has ever sounded; no colour which has ever been revealed, possibly in the darkness of oceanic depths where the eye of man has never perceived it; no wing-beat of the day-fly in far-flung epochs of geological time. Everything will be present to Him exactly as it was or is or will be, in all its reality, in the whole temporal course of its activity, in its strength or weakness, in its majesty or meanness. He will not allow anything to perish, but will hold it in the hollow of His hand as He has always done, and does, and will do.[3]

HATRED OF ONE'S ENEMIES?

Verses 19–24 of Psalm 139 bring us into the most troubling dimension of the psalms, the imprecations against one's enemies and the call for their destruction. As Christians, we do not expect invective, curses, and imprecations against our enemies to be a part of prayer to God. Most of us stumble over such parts of the psalms, or skip over them—and rightly so. Christian piety that can easily call for the destruction of enemies is fundamentally skewed and inconsistent with a true obedience to the one who commanded his followers, "Love your enemies." But these psalms with their imprecations are given to us in Scripture whether we like it or not, even with their apparent contrast to other words that we regard as basic. That means we need to struggle a bit to try to understand what is going on and what is the meaning of such words that sit in the midst of this otherwise marvelous, deep well of living water that is the Psalter.

One dimension of our discernment is the recognition that such hatred of enemies as one finds passionately expressed in this psalm and elsewhere is a part of the candor and truly painful honesty of the psalms. It reminds us that the struggles and conflicts are real, that the threats and oppression lying behind the cries to God were not just manifestations of the inconveniences of life but real hurt and terror and pain. People reacted before God with all the feeling and fury that such treatment creates.

We are further reminded of the utter openness of the dialogue. When one is in the depths and besieged on every side and the only way out is the cry to God, there are no holds barred, no no-no, naughty words, no etiquette of proper language in crying to the Lord. Whether one should or should not think and say such thoughts, in the dialogue with God

3. Barth, *Church Dogmatics* III/3 (Edinburgh: T. & T. Clark, 1960), 89–90.

one *may* say them. Indeed that may be the only place where they may be uttered. It is probably easier for us to accept the cry of anger and hurt than the prayer for destruction of one's enemies, but such prayer *is* the cry of anger and hurt.

A very important feature of the imprecations here in Psalm 139 is the conviction of the one who prays that the enemies whose defeat and destruction are called for are not just *my* and *our* enemies but *your* enemies, that is, God's enemies. It is on that ground that the psalmist calls for divine action, and the point is an important one. The issue for the psalmist is not just a matter of one's own enemies, although the element of self-interest is clearly there and is indeed the grounds for the cry for help. The one in need is also aligning herself or himself with the purpose and direction of God and in opposition to that to which God is opposed.

There are two dangers we face as we assess such a perspective. One is an easy appropriation of such a view, so that one never allows for the mistaken judgment that our enemies are God's enemies when they may be only *our* enemies—for ideological reasons or out of sinful human hatred (these may be one and the same thing). The fact that we experience hostility toward ourselves from others and so regard them as inimical to our well being, that is, as our enemies, does not automatically mean that they are inimical and opposed to God.

It is necessary also, however, to guard against the danger of thinking that God has no enemies, no opposition. That simply is not true. Even from the New Testament—and the cross may mean *especially* from the New Testament—we hear that the last enemy is death. The struggle with that enemy is the toughest of all. It has taken the most out of God, even God's own beloved Child. But there are other forces and persons who have opposed the will and purpose of God, who are inimical to God's intention to establish a rule of justice and mercy, of peace and love. There will always be those who stand against righteousness, and the psalms may be more honest and accurate than we in recognizing in such ones the enemies of God. When the psalmist declares

> I hate them with perfect hatred;
>   I count them my enemies,

there is implicit a claim that in God's creation there is a moral order that is not to be ignored and a divine purpose with which the psalmist will identify, placing himself or herself totally and implacably in opposition to whatever forces would thwart that purpose and create a way of injustice, unrighteousness, and oppression. The psalmist stands utterly against such a way and those who would walk it, saying in effect, I count them my enemies because they are inimical to your loving and just purposes.

Part of our contemporary difficulty in dealing with such expressions as we find at the end of Psalm 139 and what they suggest about the divine perspective is that we have difficulty knowing quite what to do with the judgment and anger of God except to wonder who is going to be judged and especially if we are going to be among those who experience judgment. Much of the problematic that people experience with the Old Testament lies in the fact that it has a lot of judgment and punishment in it. All the curses and imprecations against enemies are a part of that. It sounds very much as if Archie Bunker of *All in the Family* is correct: God zaps people to get even.

It is not possible, however, to get rid of judgment by excising the imprecations from the psalms or even by ignoring or letting go of the Old Testament. The ultimate act of judgment against all God's enemies is in the cross, and there is no way the judgment of God can be stepped over at that point. There it goes right to the heart of God. Nor is the judgment of God a totally negative word that we hear. It is an aspect of God's positive purposes. In some ways the best guide to what is happening in the judgment of God is those texts that show the judgment of God as a purifying, renewing, reclaiming process. This is seen for example in the image of the plumb line (2 Kings 21:13; Isa. 28:17; 34:11; Amos 7:7–9), which portrays the Lord's measuring of a nation or people or city to see if it is built straight and true, thus able to carry out the purpose for which the Lord has built or created it. If not, then the structure must be torn down, that is, judged, in order that God may start afresh to build a "true" people. A similar image occurs in 2 Kings 21:13, that of Jerusalem as a dirty dish that is wiped clean, that is, judged, not purely in retribution, but that the dish may be restored to its proper state and ready again for God's use. Fire imagery is fairly common in biblical pictures of divine destruction, but in Isa. 1:21–31 the fire is not a consuming fire but the fiery wrath of God that smelts away the impurities or sins of the people and refines them into the pure and unalloyed metal they needed to be to accomplish God's purpose. The anger and judgment of God, therefore, are not manifestations of a divine arbitrariness nor purely retribution for misdeeds, though the latter is clearly a part of the biblical understanding of judgment. Rather, God moves against people and forces—including the Lord's own people—in a way that is consistent with the divine character and purpose. Whatever is inimical to God's way of justice and mercy is the enemy of God, and divine judgment is in order to maintain the just and merciful way.[4]

One final word needs to be said for our understanding and appropriation of these imprecations. Vengeance belongs to *God*. It really does—which takes it totally out of our hands. The human word that calls for God's judgment or vengeance cannot become the human deed of vengeance. The prayer for God's vengeance is once again the prayer for God's will to be done. Vengeance in the Old Testament is *vindication*, vindication of the purpose of God.[5] It is the manifestation of justice and moral order, not a cruel annihilation of certain persons or peoples for the sake of revenge or retaliation. Vengeance in the Old Testament vocabulary is the language to express what the prophets meant by the plumb line—God's move to right the human situation.[6]

4. "In one sense the enemies of Yahweh are unmasked as his purposes in history are revealed and there are seen to be men who stand against the fulfillment of those purposes. Or again, the specific claims of Yahweh's holiness are made known and there are seen to be enemies who stand against those claims" (James Wharton, " 'Smitten of God . . .': A Theological Investigation of the Enemies of Yahweh in the Old Testament," *Austin Seminary Bulletin* 76 (1960): 13.

5. See George E. Mendenhall on "The 'Vengeance' of Yahweh," in *The Tenth Generation* (Baltimore: Johns Hopkins Univ. Press, 1973), 69–104.

6. For an excellent treatment of vengeance in the psalms, see Walter Brueggemann, on "Vengeance: Human and Divine" in *Praying the Psalms* (Winona, Minn.: St. Mary's Press, 1982), 67–80.

RESOURCES FOR
FURTHER STUDY

TRANSLATIONS

There are, in addition to the standard translations of the Old Testament, many separate translations of the psalms. The usefulness of these is often very much a matter of personal choice or response. They may be very helpful, especially in one's devotional life. For more extensive interpretation, however, I would recommend the use of the standard translations such as Revised Standard Version (RSV), New English Bible (NEB), Jerusalem Bible (JB), New American Bible (NAB), the new Jewish Publication Society version (JPS), and Today's English Version (TEV, commonly known as The Good News Bible). I find it often helpful to use the RSV as my base translation, one that represents a fairly formal translation of the Hebrew text, and compare that with a more dynamic translation, such as TEV, to get another idea about how the thought of a line or verse may be expressed. For example, the line in Psalm 23 translated by RSV as, "thou anointest my head with oil," is helpfully translated by TEV as "You treat me as an honored guest." One translation points us to the actual practice of an ancient host. The other suggests what it means. The interpreter does not have to choose (though sometimes translation choices have to be made when there are true conflicts or misunderstandings); both translations are helpful.

A warning is in order about the use of translations. The proliferation of contemporary translations is not all blessing. One of its results is a tendency on the part of the interpreters to think that comparing more and more translations is helpful. It is not! There is a clear law of diminishing returns. Time is wasted as one searches several translations. Often information is collected, but it remains merely data, not useful. Choose a couple of translations that you know are generally reliable and of a somewhat different character, that is, one more formal or literal, one more dynamic, getting at the idea communicated. Where possible and necessary check them against the Hebrew or a commentary. Control of the Hebrew text is indeed helpful for getting at the meaning of a text. At the same time it must be said that ability to use the Hebrew Bible is not a necessity for the faithful preaching and teaching of the psalms in the congregation.

COMMENTARIES

Contemporary Commentaries. Few books of the Old Testament have been the subject of as many commentaries as the psalms. Here are some that I have found useful:

Artur Weiser. *The Psalms.* Old Testament Library. Philadelphia: Westminster Press, 1962. This has been a standard commentary for over twenty years, and for many persons it has been the most helpful. The comments are generally non-technical and of an expository character. It is sometimes overly controlled by a cultic interpretation that is set forth in the introduction and referred to frequently. Users of the commentary should treat those references lightly.

J. W. Rogerson and J. W. McKay. *Psalms 1—50. Psalms 51—100. Psalms 101—150.* Cambridge Bible Commentary. Cambridge: Cambridge Univ. Press, 1977. These three volumes are based on the New English Bible. They are essentially notes on words and phrases, but the authors are often perceptive in their comments and give a brief general outline and interpretation of each psalm.

J. H. Eaton. *Psalms.* Torch Bible Commentaries. London: SCM Press, 1967. This work is similar in size, scope, and character to the preceding. A useful, small, one-volume commentary characterized by a strong and often effective argument for seeing many psalms as composed for the king.

A. A. Anderson. *Psalms 1—72. Psalms 73—150.* New Century Bible Commentary. Grand Rapids: Wm. B. Eerdmans, 1972. Here is a much more technical collection of notes on the Pslams. The reader is not given much help at getting a good sense of the whole. The treatment tends to be atomistic. Much information is given, however, and the chief contribution of the commentary is its summary reference to much of the contemporary literature and scholarly perspective on the psalms.

P. C. Craigie. *Psalms 1—50.* L. C. Allen. *Psalms 101—150.* Word Biblical Commentary. Waco, Tex.: Word Books, 1983. This is the most recent and, in some respects, the best of the scholarly commentaries on the psalms. Its chief weaknesses are a certain unevenness of approach that is inevitable with different authors and the fact that the middle volume on Psalms 51—100 is not yet published. Craigie and Allen furnish an up-to-date bibliography and discuss textual, grammatical, and syntactic matters in a set of notes to each psalm. Craigie, especially, provides a sensitive and helpful elaboration of the meaning of each psalm. He gives attention to New Testament relationships as well. His volume should be quite useful to the preacher and teacher. I recommend it. Allen's approach is different. He gives much more attention to form, structure, and setting with constant reference to contemporary literature. He also has a good feel for literary and aesthetic dimensions of the psalms. These are the strengths of his volume. He is less effective at pulling everything together into a whole, though even at that level his commentary is useful.

Leopold Sabourin. *The Psalms: Their Origin and Meaning.* 2 vols. Staten Island, N.Y.: Alba House, 1969. These volumes contain a brief and very sketchy treatment of each psalm. They are most useful to one who knows Hebrew and contain many references to contemporary literature. The chief characteristic and virtue is the arrangement of the psalms by their type or genre. That does, however, make this commentary somewhat more difficult to use.

Mitchell Dahood. *Psalms.* 3 vols. Anchor Bible. Garden City, N.Y.: Doubleday & Co., 1965, 1968, 1970. This is a widely publicized work by the late great Ugaritic scholar. It is of little use to anyone without an advanced knowledge of Northwest Semitic languages. The biblical text is constantly modified and often wrongly so. Let the reader beware.

Samuel Terrien. *The Psalms and Their Meaning for Today.* New York: Bobbs-Merrill, 1952. Not technically a commentary, Terrien's book was written to give the general reader a picture of the psalms' "original purpose, contents, religious truth, poetic beauty, and significance." Many psalms are given full and valuable expositions. I have found it quite helpful.

Walter Brueggemann. *The Message of the Psalms: A Theological Commentary.* Minneapolis: Augsburg Pub. House, 1984. This recent commentary by a gifted communicator of the message of the Old Testament and its relevance to our life and times offers a fresh, readable commentary on about sixty psalms. Highly recommended.

John Goldingay. *Songs from a Strange Land: Psalms 42—51.* Downers Grove, Ill.: Inter-Varsity Press, 1978. Though this small volume by an able evangelical scholar deals only with ten psalms, it is one of the better commentaries available on these psalms. Goldingay puts together linguistic and theological acumen with a concern for the relation of the text to questions about human existence and Christian life.

Older Commentaries. We tend to forget or ignore these valuable resources.

Luther's Works. Vols. 10 and 11, *First Lectures on the Psalms.* Vols. 12–14, *Selected Psalms.* St. Louis: Concordia Pub. House, 1955–74. The *First Lectures* contain individual notes on each psalm. They are uneven, often treating three or four works or verses in a long psalm. The *Selected Psalms* provide a coverage of the whole of each psalm taken up. The treatment is sometimes sketchy but Luther's vigorous grasp of the power of the psalms as well as his theological emphasis come through; they are to be read critically and appreciatively. An excellent treatment of Luther's interpretation of the psalms as a key to his hermeneutical development is given in James S. Preus, *From Shadow to Promise* (Cambridge: Harvard Univ. Press, 1969).

Calvin's Commentaries. Psalms. 5 vols. Grand Rapids: Wm. B. Eerdmans, 1949. John Calvin was one of the great exegetes, and his commentaries remain a valuable resource. He is able to comprehend the basic meaning of a text as it arises out of grammar, syntax, and the meaning of words in context. While christological interpretations generally are not forced, royal psalms as well as others are heard in the light of the revelation of God in Jesus Christ. Many contemporary commentaries do not move significantly beyond Calvin in getting a fundamental grasp of the text.

F. Delitzsch. *Psalms.* Vol. 5 of *Commentary on the Old Testament,* by C. F. Keil and F. Delitzsch. Reprint. Grand Rapids: Wm. B. Eerdmans, 1980. J. J. Stewart Perowne. *The Book of Psalms.* Reprint of 1878 edition. Grand Rapids: Zondervan Pub. House, 1976. A. F. Kirkpatrick. *The Book of Psalms.* Reprint of 1902 edition. Cambridge Bible. Cambridge: Cambridge Univ. Press, 1951. All three of these commentaries were written in the nineteenth century or at the turn of the century (Kirkpatrick). All have been reprinted for good reason. They are rich commentaries by able scholars who knew the psalms well and gave attention to substantive matters in their comment. Each of them discusses the text in terms of an understanding of its component parts or structure. The reader is given a sense of the whole and the way the parts relate to each other to express the communication of the psalm. Kirkpatrick does not refer to the Hebrew, though he clearly bases his interpretation on an understanding of the Hebrew and corrects the translation used in the Cambridge Bible series. Perowne deals with difficult matters in the Hebrew text in a separate section at the end of his comment on each psalm. Delitzsch integrates all his comments into a single running commentary. Judgments about dating and authorship are often questionable in these commentaries, but that is true of more recent works also, and here they do not occupy too much attention. All three commentaries are of enduring value.

GENERAL AND THEOLOGICAL WORKS

Othmar Keel. *The Symbolism of the Biblical World: Ancient Near Eastern Iconography and the Book of Psalms.* New York: Seabury Press, 1978. This is an unusual and very interesting book on the psalms. Keel provides what is in effect a visual commentary on the psalms arranged by theme and topic rather than psalm number. There are nearly 500 illustrations from the art of the ancient Near East that do in fact illustrate themes, verses, and words from the psalms. Extended commentary explains the relation of the illustrations to the psalms. An index allows one to find the illustrations pertaining to any particular psalm. A veritable gold mine of visual images bringing the psalms to life.

Claus Westermann. *Praise and Lament in the Psalms.* Atlanta: John Knox Press, 1981. A landmark volume in the contemporary study of the psalms, this book is basic for understanding the forms of lament and praise. Especially valuable is Westermann's final chapter on the theology of the lament.

Claus Westermann. *The Psalms: Structure, Content, and Message.* Minneapolis: Augsburg Pub. House, 1980. Here is an excellent small introduction to the psalms in terms of their basic types.

B. W. Anderson. *Out of the Depths: The Psalms Speak for Us Today.* Rev. ed. Philadelphia: Westminster Press, 1983. While similar to the preceding in its approach to the psalms in terms of their types, this book deals with more of them and is helpful in getting at their theology. It is a useful study book.

R. Murphy. *The Psalms, Job.* Proclamation Commentaries. Philadelphia: Fortress Press, 1977. Not really a commentary, the psalms section of this book has chapters on the types, theological themes, and the contribution of the psalms to our understanding of prayer.

W. Brueggemann. *Praying the Psalms.* Winona, Minn.: St. Mary's Press, 1982. Brueggemann presents five essays on the language and imagery of the psalms, their relation to human experience, the "Jewishness" of the psalms, and the problem of vengeance. The last essay is especially helpful on a problem that perplexes many Christians. The latter half of the book reprints the RSV text of the Psalter.

C. S. Lewis. *Reflections on the Psalms.* New York: Harcourt, Brace & Co., 1958. In his inimitable style Lewis takes up issues and aspects of the psalms in a fresh way. He focuses on difficult matters and demonstrates why he was one of the great apologists for Christian faith in our time. I find it especially helpful on the tough and troubling questions.

Harvey H. Guthrie. *Israel's Sacred Psalms: A Study of Dominant Themes.* New York: Seabury Press, 1966; idem, *Theology as Thanksgiving.* New York: Seabury Press, 1981. The titles of these two works aptly describe their contents. The second volume is especially helpful on the relation of psalms to liturgy.

Interpretation 28/1 (1974) and *Interpretation* 39/1 (1985). These two issues of the journal *Interpretation* are devoted to the lament (1974) and the hymn of praise (1985). They are not confined to the psalms, but the psalms are the primary focus of the articles.

Karl Barth. *Church Dogmatics.* 14 vols. Edinburgh: T. & T. Clark, 1936–77. This may seem to be a surprising item in a psalms bibliography, but Barth was a first-class exegete and his *Church Dogmatics* is a rich mine of exegetical insights that should be in the library of every biblical interpreter. The index volume is a must in order to locate his exegetical sections, which range from a line or two to several pages of small print.

THE PSALMS IN WORSHIP AND LIFE

S. Mowinckel. *The Psalms in Israel's Worship*. 2 vols. Nashville: Abingdon Press, 1962. This is one of the great works of this century on the psalms. Many subjects are treated, but Mowinckel was especially interested in the relation of the psalms to the cult, and the liturgy and worship of ancient Israel.

M. H. Shepherd, Jr. *The Psalms in Christian Worship: A Practical Guide*. Minneapolis: Augsburg Pub. House, 1976. This eminent liturgiologist offers us an excellent guidebook as to how the psalms have been used in liturgy and musical adaptations. A bibliography at the end identifies a number of musical settings of the psalms.

R. E. Prothero. *The Psalms in Human Life*. London: John Murray, 1904. Written at the turn of the century, this book is a rich collection of notes and stories on how the psalms have been drawn upon in history from the church fathers to the twentieth century—from Augustine and Jerome, through Wyclif, Hus, and Richard Hooker, down to Benjamin Franklin, the Wesleys, William Wilberforce, and David Livingstone. A great store of useful illustrations of the place of the psalms in human experience are to be found in it.

John Ker. *The Psalms in History and Biography*. New York: Robert Carter, 1886. Also an older work (nineteenth century), Ker's book is similar to Prothero's in seeking to provide illustrations from history of the use of the psalms. It is much briefer and is arranged according to psalms rather than chronologically like Prothero's.

Donald L. Griggs. *Praying and Teaching the Psalms*. Nashville: Abingdon Press, 1984. The title accurately describes this useful book. Half of the book suggests activities to help persons learn to pray the psalms, and half offers activities for teaching the psalms, primarily in terms of their types. Anyone who teaches the psalms in a congregation and to varying age groups should find the book helpful.

SCRIPTURE INDEX

OLD TESTAMENT

NEW TESTAMENT

INDEX OF AUTHORS